PROPERTY OF
GAVIN SMITH

MW00397348

EDWARD S. LISK

The MUSICAL MIND *of the* CREATIVE DIRECTOR

Published by
Meredith Music Publications
a division of G.W. Music, Inc.
4899 Lerch Creek Ct., Galesville, MD 20765
http://www.meredithmusic.com

MEREDITH MUSIC PUBLICATIONS and its stylized double M logo
are trademarks of
MEREDITH MUSIC PUBLICATIONS, a division of G.W. Music, Inc.

No part of this book may be reproduced or transmitted in any form or by any means, electronic or mechanical, including photocopying, recording, or by any informational storage or retrieval system without permission in writing
from the publisher.

While every effort has been made to trace copyright holders and obtain permission,
this has not been possible in all cases; any omissions brought to our attention will be remedied
in future editions.

Copyright © 2010 MEREDITH MUSIC PUBLICATIONS
International Copyright Secured • All Rights Reserved
First Edition
September 2010

International Standard Book Number: 978-1-57463-160-9
Cataloging-in-Publication Data is on file with the Library of Congress.
Library of Congress Control Number: 2010925719
Printed and bound in U.S.A.

IN SUPPORT OF THE CREATIVE DIRECTOR SERIES...

"The writings and publications of Ed Lisk represent the very best rehearsal and performance pedagogy to be found in our profession. His advice is golden and, once employed, can often be life altering. In person, as a clinician, his teachings simply come alive and there is no one better as a mentor and role model for instrumental teachers and conductors."

DR. JOHN R. LOCKE, *Director of Bands, Professor, University of North Carolina at Greensboro; Editor, The Journal of Band Research*

"As a musician and teacher, Ed Lisk explores the very heart of ensemble music making. His approach is both scholarly and artistic, fluently crossing the abyss between the technical and the musical, providing a valuable resource for the development of ensemble musicians. A highly recommended resource for any conductor, teacher, and musician!"

DR. MARK FONDER, *Professor, Conductor, Ithaca College Concert Band, School of Music, Ithaca College*

"Ed Lisk is without question a master teacher, unselfish mentor, and first and foremost a musician of knowledge. The books he has authored on rehearsals, pedagogy, and organization reveal and explain many mysteries of musicianship. His knowledge should be required reading for the college music education major and definitely be found on every teacher's bookshelf."

MARK KELLY, *Director of Bands Emeritus, Bowling Green State University*

"Ed Lisk lives what he writes and shares his beauty and wonder-filled world of Music-making and Teaching. Ed offers yet another journal in his life-spanning experiences, his vast intuitions, sensibilities and poignant understanding of Music and its bequeathing to the generations that follow. As we share in his forever young look at Music, so too do we grow in our maturing understanding of a virtually limitless language. Godspeed."

STEPHEN MELILLO, *Composer*

"At a time of dramatic educational and societal change, when thinking and values of the past have been cast aside, Ed Lisk has established himself as a unique leader in the profession. The ideas he expresses, and continues to express, through his writings, lectures, and clinics are not based on current trends of sentiment, emotion, or commercialism, but rather on the time-honored traditions of intellect, experience, and reason. His ideas and methods are utilized daily by hundreds of band directors throughout the nation. And it is making a difference—for teachers, students, and all who care about music and the musical experience for young people. Ed's contribution to the profession is beyond measure and his integrity as an educator is beyond reproach."

BOBBY ADAMS, *Ph.D., Director of Bands, Stetson University*

"Ed Lisk is singularly one of the most remarkable pedagogical minds in our profession today. His concise prose, combined with a thoroughly researched, uniquely logical, and analytical approach to all aspects of the musical process, make any Lisk publication an eagerly awaited and thoroughly enlightening event. Ed Lisk's books should be required reading for all serious music educators."

> PAULA A. CRIDER, *Director Emeritus, University of Texas Band, Austin, TX*

"Edward Lisk goes beyond mere study of knowledge and skill and delves deep into musical understandings and expression, allowing teachers and students to truly discover the beauty of music."

> ELIZABETH SOKOLOWSKI, *Chair of Music Education, University of the Arts, Philadelphia, PA*

"Ed Lisk, in his new book *The Musical Mind of the Creative Director*, has taken the reader from a methodical approach of teaching the fundamentals of music in rehearsal to the finished product, a well-planned musical performance. If you follow Lisk's approach from the *Creative Director* to *The Musical Mind of the Creative Director*, it will greatly improve not only your ensemble's performance but also the way you think about music."

> DENNIS ZEISLER, *Director of Bands, Old Dominion University, Norfolk, Virginia*

"*The Musical Mind of the Creative Director* is a must-read and must-have text for the truly informed wind-band scholar. This is an indispensable resource that is a new addition to the Creative Director Series. The entire series belongs in every wind band library."

> RICHARD MILES, *Editor and Compiler of the Teaching Music through Performance in Band Series*

"The Creative Director Series delves into the very essence of the wind band and celebrates all of the best qualities that the wind band has brought to our culture as a valid musical institution. As an educational reference, it provides the wind band conductor with time-tested musical craftsmanship techniques, profound intellectual discussions centered around musical artistry, and reflections on how and why people learn, emphasizing the richness that musical experiences bring to this learning. Presented with a level of style and elegance that is characteristic of Edward Lisk himself, The Creative Director Series belongs prominently on the bookshelf of every wind band conductor."

> THOMAS E. REYNOLDS, *Conductor, Massachusetts Institute of Technology Concert Band, Cambridge, Massachusetts*

"All I can say is WOW. This MUST be required reading for all college pedagogy courses. The information you give for the young and one-day insightful conductors is profound. Your clear demonstration and explanations on how to make a 'good' ensemble great are incredible. You give light to where those teachers at times do not even look and you instill within your writing a calm demeanor and sense of purpose. As a leader, you give us enormous and helpful tools for music education advocacy. It is just incredible stuff. If there were a band bible it would be this book to open it up. So many things that I had a hard time understanding/being explained to me have been cleared up! Bravo! Thanks again Ed; it's so easy to LOVE learning by reading such great, clear, and concise material. Thank you for inspiring me to be a teacher."

WALTER F. AVELLANEDA, *Jr., Composer*

"Thank you for sharing your system of musical learning with all of those who are willing to take the risk of getting better. Your system of teaching scales, beatless tuning, and the use of internal pulse has developed individual and ensemble technique, as well as a tonal beauty in our band sound that allows my students to perform music that at one time was out of their reach. I'm only telling you these things because what you are teaching works, and the students and parents, as well as myself, at Spring-Ford Area High School are extremely indebted to you and you dedication in spreading this message. Your techniques have transformed a very ordinary band program into an extraordinary program!"

JOHN ECKSTINE, *Director of Bands, Spring-Ford High School, Pennsylvania*

PROPERTY OF
GAVIN SMITH

Contents

PREFACE

I remember so clearly my first rehearsal as a new band director, back in the early part of my career. It was an intimidating and humbling experience to stand before my very first class of high school students, all looking to me for instruction. I had very high expectations, as many of these musicians had begun lessons in fourth grade, and so had several years of practice in study. The rehearsal began. I was nervous but made sure that I had the 4/4 conducting pattern under control, so that they could "follow me." What a surprise was in store for me! The best description for this rehearsal would be "train wreck."

We started again from the beginning. This time it should work, I thought. Surprise, surprise. Another crash. Nervous and searching for a solution, the wheels began to spin in my mind. I was doing what I was taught to do in college, in my preparation to become a band director: Conduct carefully, follow the pattern, and the band will follow. But this technique wasn't working! It was at this point—on my first day on the job—that I realized what doesn't work. All I had to do was to find out why.

And so, the search and research began. I devoted my career to observing the finest conductors and studying countless books about teaching, psychology, and music philosophy. I consumed many hours observing the legends of our profession . . . Frederick Fennell, Donald Hunsberger, Harry Begian, Frank Battisti, Col. Gabriel, John Paynter, Donald McGinnis, and James Croft are just but a few. I was determined to find the best way to have a successful program.

As my early band program developed, I began to realize that the traditional techniques were causing problems for the students. When I questioned some of my band director friends, I always received an answer that placed the blame on the students: that they most likely were not practicing. However, my observations were different. In observing various band programs and directors, what came to my attention was that many directors were doing the same thing in rehearsals, with varied results. They were simply following a "formula"—for example, playing a Bb concert scale and a brief chorale followed by the literature to be prepared. Surprisingly, these rehearsals were boring, even to me, an interested observer. I can't imagine what the students were thinking about in this type of rehearsal setting.

It was at this point in my career that I decided to depart from the traditional rehearsal format, and began to develop my own method, which I came to call "Alternative Rehearsal Techniques." These techniques were my way of finding solutions to "things" that I believed hampered my student's progress. Sharing those solutions is the driving force behind this book.

INTRODUCTION

In my quest to provide an optimum experience for my students over my fifty-plus years as a musician and educator, I have read countless research documents addressing a nearly infinite range of instrumental topics. Most focus on methods and formulas that determine student achievement. But interestingly, very few focus on the instructional delivery system—that is, instructional and rehearsal techniques based on fundamental concepts that are connected to what was previously learned.

This is unfortunate, because the instructional delivery system determines just how good—or how bad—your ensemble will perform. Many directors are in search of a "success formula" or finding the correct method book that will solve all the ills of their program. This will never happen, however, because there is no single, external solution.

Many publications have been written regarding conducting, score analysis, phrasing, musical expression, balance, blend, intonation, and the list continues. There are as many ways to deal with musical issues as there are professors, clinicians, conductors, and teachers practicing currently—and some methods and techniques are superior to others. What is most important is that one implements those practices that produce the expected musical results, and that we question the techniques that hamper student progress. Too often directors follow the old cliché, "But this is the way we've been doing it for years..."

Well, frankly, some of those techniques don't work. This issue has troubled me throughout my career. I constantly questioned many of the traditional approaches, as I believed so many actually delayed musical growth and achievement.

In my career, I have had the good fortune to observe many "legends" of the band world, in hopes of peeking inside their minds to see what they were thinking about, what they were listening to, and how they were making musical decisions about what they were conducting. Moreover, I wondered, where were their musical feelings originating from, and what determined their interpretation and stylistic considerations in shaping the uniqueness of a performance? Certainly, they demonstrated an in-depth harmonic and melodic understanding of every piece they conducted, as well as an extensive awareness of the historical background of any given piece.

But there is more to it, I discovered. How do they decide which interpretation is acceptable or correct? Does it come with age and experience? As a young conductor I was cautious as to what musical liberties I would take. At my current age, with so many years of experience, I have no fear regarding the risks I take with musical styling and interpretation. So, how did I achieve this confidence?

What I've learned is that the ultimate success formula for any band lies within the individual director. Notable researcher Dr. Cliff Madsen at Florida State University, states, "Trust the process of growth and not the formula." My own growth has stemmed from careful study the psychology of learning, the psychology of music, and the natural learning process, from Plato to Piaget, Maslow, Howard Gardner's Multiple Intelligences, and brain-based learning. Couple this with the writings of Aaron Copland, Leonard Bernstein, Pablo Casals, William Kincaid, Elizabeth Green, Percy Grainger, John Sloboda, James Jordan, Mortimer Adler, Robert Sternberg, Bennett Reimer, David Elliott, and Mihaly Csikszentmihalyi—but a few of the musical thinkers that "fuel" my library and knowledge base. Such a varied reading list quickly amplifies a director's understanding of just how comprehensive is musical learning and its magnificent importance for young students.

This study, combined with a half century as a professional musician, conductor, and teacher, forms the foundation for my assertions in this volume and the *Creative Director* series: musical learning is not just about elevating a student's technical skills. True musical education is about enhancing a musician's performance level through alerting their minds to the beauty of musical expression.

My intentions in this book are straightforward: to share with you an approach and a series of key exercises that will foster in your music students a greater awareness of the many components that surround the beauty of musical expression. These techniques are based on extensive research that includes reviews of the literature, observation of the "legends" in the field, and personal experience. My techniques have been field-tested in my own classrooms, with students ranging from ages 10 to 70, and also by countless other educators who have tried the techniques themselves and who have enthusiastically told me of their success.

The concepts and instructional techniques presented here have been implemented by many band programs, and this volume solidifies the entire system of musical learning. This volume complements my work in previous publications, with a fresh look at topics covered in earlier volumes in the *Creative Director* series, all available from Meredith Music Publications. Herein, I have expanded many of the concepts to illustrate the depth and connections that complement student and director learning.

My professional tenure and travels have allowed me to address thousands of instrumental music educators in workshops, clinics, and in lectures all over the United States. Inevitably, this has resulted in hours of informed questions and thoughtful discussion that have provided valuable insight as to the strengths and weaknesses of various methods within our teaching profession. The reality is that there is very little written in the music education literature that addresses the specifics of a teacher delivery system as found in the *Creative Director* series—but I have found educators and musicians very eager to discuss it. And, perhaps more importantly, I have realized that no understanding of musicianship is complete without it.

This publication is intended to further open your eyes to the vast universe of the world of music that we are engaged in. My intention is to share with you a proven way to think about music, teach music, play music, and conduct music—giving you an approach that ensures student and program success, a creative approach to creating and experience music: a new dimension in teaching, thinking, practicing, and playing an instrument.

HOW THIS BOOK IS ORGANIZED

This book presents to you my Alternative Rehearsal Techniques hand-in-hand with thoughts on the musician and the musician's mind, both from the perspective of the music director, the ensemble, and the individual musician.

We begin in chapter 1 by looking inside how a musician's mind functions to catch a glimpse into the complexities of what it is that we do. Each chapter then covers a critical band teaching topic, providing reflections on the musical experience both for the conductor and the student, alongside exercises you can do in your classroom to build students' skills in rhythm, expression, dynamics, articulation, balance, blend, intonation, and overall tone quality and sonority. In the appendices, I provide additional activities and exercises, excerpted from other books in my *Creative Director* series.

CHAPTER 1.

THE IMMERSED MUSICAL MIND

The success of an ensemble stems from a fundamental concept: teaching students to make quality musical decisions. The quality of their musical decisions is the primary determining factor in the quality of an ensemble's performance. Our rehearsal and instructional techniques must be presented in a way that holds students responsible for their musical product. When a director attempts to make the decisions for an ensemble, students become passive and conditioned into waiting to be told what to do. The results will always be evident during a performance.

Notable scholar, author, and educator Mortimer Adler makes a powerful statement in his 1988 publication, *Reforming Education:* "The primary cause of learning is the activity of the student's mind. The best that the best teacher can do is to assist that activity."

I was amazed how much my students improved when I anticipated how they perceived musical expectations. As I instructed the students, I anticipated their thoughts on how they would respond musically to my directions. An error-free response indicated that my directions were clearly understood. Just as important, did my students understand what was presented and were they able to apply this learning to other situations? The ability to transfer new learning to other circumstances and environments is key to student cognition of content and concepts.

When I teach young students, I ask many questions but inform them not to give me a verbal answer; I will "hear" the answer in their music making. For example, if we are working on scales, I may ask the question, "What is the key signature for the F# major scale?" The student would respond by playing the F# major scale (error free).

Always, the results are determined by your teaching techniques. If you don't hear what you taught the students, it is obvious that the instruction created the misunderstanding. Too often, directors ask questions and proceed if they hear the correct *verbal* answer, but what they really should be listening for is the *musical* answer. More often than not, the musical result has not changed or improved.

Our teaching techniques must place all the responsibilities on the student and their decision-making processes. They must have complete control of what comes out of their instrument. The guided teaching strategies provided in this book elevate thinking and response for immediate improvement.

METACOGNITION

Three educational concepts provide support for involving students in the decision making process: metacognition, connected learning, and orchestrated immersion. The purpose of these teaching techniques is to totally consume the students in the musical process so that their music making is not a technical activity but rather engages their mind actively in the process. For example, I teach that there are three aspects of tone quality: balance, blend, and intonation. One of my favorite statements is to state, "If you hear yourself, one of three things is happening: you are overblowing (balance), you are playing with poor tone quality (blend), or you are not in tune (intonation)." By paying attention to these three factors themselves, the students become totally immersed in listening and the results are overwhelming and stun directors.

By actively engaging the students' minds in the musical result, they are no longer bored with what they believe to be superficial activities. In my own classes, frequently it was a surprise when the bell rang to indicate the end of a period, as we were so consumed with the process of music making that we never realized how much time had passed. The intensity of concentration was from the beginning of the rehearsal to the end. This only comes from being totally immersed in what is happening.

The activities we will explore in subsequent chapters nurture this kind of engagement in a process I refer to as metacognition. Metacognition is defined as a state of awareness (thinking) that occurs as we perform specific tasks, and determines how we apply this awareness to control what we are doing. The perfect example of metacognition is in the statement made earlier, "If you hear yourself, one of three things is happening." The student then must apply what he or she knows, and adjust his or her playing accordingly. Without reservation, such awareness is the essential ingredient for a successful band director and band program, and the activities in subsequent chapters all develop this sort of immersive engagement.

Renate and Geoffrey Caine in their book, *Making Connections: Teaching and the Human Brain,* present three instructional techniques that ensure total immersion in the learning process:

- orchestrated immersion
- relaxed alertness
- active processing

Each is defined as follows:

Orchestrated immersion: Orchestrated immersion refers to learning situations that fully immerse learners in an educational experience, and this depends on the ability of the teacher to present information and bring it to life in the minds of the students. Orchestrated immersion provides students with a rich and complex experience. Retention levels are increased and helps student to establish patterns and associations making learning more permanent.

Relaxed alertness: Relaxed alertness means that we have eliminated fear in learners, while maintaining a highly challenging environment. Relaxed alertness ensures that students are being challenged within a context of safety (no threats, rules, or regulations if something is not done). It also includes a personal sense of wellbeing that allows students to explore new thoughts and connections.

Active processing: Active processing means consolidating and internalizing information by the learner in a way that is personally meaningful and coherent. It is the path to understanding, rather than simply to memory. Active processing engages emotions, concepts, and values. The brain searches to form meaningful patterns from experiences. The associations set up permanent learning before grasping the new information and storing it for further use.

These techniques apply very readily to music teaching. Efficient and successful music teaching techniques based upon orchestrated immersion, relaxed alertness, and active processing elevate a student's learning and performance skills to levels beyond most conventional approaches. When a director has command of such instructional methods, the ensemble's musical potential increases significantly.

Just as important as the student's immersion is the director's immersion. Observe any concert and conductor; it is quickly apparent when a conductor is totally immersed in an ensemble's music performance. If this "immersion" does not exist between conductor and ensemble, we often hear an "exercise" which sounds removed from musical meaning. In contrast, when a conductor is immersed into music making, *the score is no longer necessary*, only the music in its entirety, as produced by the ensemble. The conductor is consumed with the "now"—this very moment of music making and no other.

Psychologists refer to this type of immersion as being the summit experience, self-actualization, or peak experience. Young inexperienced directors can find it difficult to depart from the score. Correcting errors and listening for mistakes frequently consume an entire rehearsal, often with no attention paid whatsoever to teaching students to make expressive music. It takes years of teaching and conducting for some directors to let go of traditional methods and become comfortable enough to instead focus attention on expressive music making.

Many regard expressive music making as an advanced activity that should only come after technical mastery. But in my opinion, students can be taught expression from Day 1. The life of a musician often begins at an early age. Musical practice is a secluded, solitary discipline, as one practices hour after hour alone in a practice space. It is very different from what other students are consumed, with either in school time or during their spare time. (We'll look at expressive music making more in chapters 4, 5, 6, and 7.)

What is it that occurs in a musician's mind? Playing a musical instrument requires an intricate combination of intellectual, visual, physical, and auditory control coupled with a perceptive decision-making process . . . what I refer to as **intelligence in action**. When conducting or playing an instrument, our mind is consumed/immersed in the sounds being created with a spontaneous response to key, rhythm, harmonic content, tempo, style, interpretation, and everything pertaining to the creation of composition. The perceptive decision-making process builds on concepts taught in the past to enhance students' performance, both now and in the future. It is based on past, present, and future: the style and interpretation of what was created (past), the style and interpretation of what is being created (present), and the style and interpretation what will be created (future). If the musician's mind changes focus, the results of the performance are distorted and no longer worthy of acceptance.

Dr. Frank Wilson, notable neurologist, reported at the 1993-94 Nobel Peace Conference in Minneapolis that " . . . when a musician plays his instrument, he uses approximately 90 % of the brain." Wilson states, "They could find no other activity that uses the brain to this extent." McGill University Professor David Levitin states in his superb publication, *This Is Your Brain On Music* (2006), "Music listening, performance, and composition engage nearly every area of the brain that we have so far identified, and involves nearly every neural subsystem." (p. 9)

Musical practice has a pivotal effect on the development of the mind, over the long term. Practice, with its focus on musical detail, fosters patience, discipline, and intensity of thought, develops a musical mind over time, and the effect is cumulative.

With growing attention to musical detail, the musical mind continues to expand with longer hours of practice. It is only through these long hours that the mind can be so developed. There are no shortcuts to becoming a musician or conductor.

For these reasons, an instrumental music program serves as an essential component of education. The complexities of performing in an instrumental ensemble are massive. The current research and information about cognition states that the benefits of instrumental music extend far beyond the normal school learning experience. A Harvard-based study (published October 29, 2008 by Drs. Gottfried Schlaug and Ellen Winne) found that students who study a musical instrument for at least three years outperform students with no instrumental training—not only in tests of auditory discrimination and finger dexterity (skills honed by the study of a musical instrument), but also on tests measuring verbal ability and visual pattern completion (skills not normally associated with music).

Indeed, musical performance calls into action a variety of intelligences. The instrumental ensemble is a unique discipline, as it addresses the importance of inter- and intrapersonal skill (intelligence) development like no other subject or discipline. It is perhaps the only learning situation found in a school setting that allows a student to be autonomous while making musical decisions that affect the full ensemble (synergy). Howard Gardner's 1983 publication, *Frames of Mind: The Theory of Multiple Intelligences,* identifies seven intelligences. (He later expanded it to 8.5 intelligences.) Gardner's theory, originally published in 1983 and widely accepted by educators worldwide, states that his goal was to come up with a view of human thought that was broader and more comprehensive than that which was accepted in cognitive studies. Gardner theorized that there are eight and a half intelligences. These are:

1. **Musical Intelligence** involves skill in the performance, composition, and appreciation of musical patterns.
2. **Logical/Mathematical Intelligence** consists of the capacity to analyze problems logically, carry out mathematical operations, and investigate issues scientifically.
3. **Verbal/Linguistic Intelligence** involves the sensitivity to spoken and written language, the ability to learn languages, and the capacity to use language to accomplish certain goals.
4. **Visual/Spatial Intelligence** is the language of shapes, images, patterns, designs, pictures, and "inner seeing," involving such things as active imagination, pretending, and visualization.

5. **Bodily-Kinesthetic Intelligence** is the language of physical movement and involves such things as creative and interpretive dance, drama, mime, conducting, and playing a musical instrument.

6. **Interpersonal Intelligence** is concerned with the capacity to understand the intentions, motivations, and desires of other people. It allows people to work effectively with others.

7. **Intrapersonal Intelligence** is the language of introspection and awareness of internal aspects of the self, including awareness of one's own feelings, intuitions, and thinking processes.

8. **Naturalist Intelligence** is the language of natural patterns, and the external and internal sensory experience of the natural world.

9. **Existentialism** can be defined as the ability to be sensitive to, or tackle deeper or larger questions about human existence, such as the meaning of life, why are we born, why do we die, what is consciousness, or how did we get here.

Five of his intelligences play a particular role in rehearsal settings, both from the performer's perspective and from the conductor/teacher/leader's perspective.

- **Musical Intelligence** involves skill in the performance, composition, and appreciation of musical patterns. It encompasses the capacity to recognize and create musical pitches, tones, and rhythms. According to Gardner, musical intelligence runs in a similar structural parallel to linguistic intelligence. We become musicians and educators because musical intelligence was our strength and played a significant role in our education.

- **Bodily-Kinesthetic Intelligence** is the control of one's body, of objects, timing, of trained responses that function like reflexes, and the mind-body connection. Creative and interpretive conducting, playing a musical instrument, gesturing, body language, and facial expression are key components of this intelligence. A few of the musical techniques and elements encompassed in this intelligence are articulation, scales (finger feeling of key tonality), complex fingering patterns, trills, and embellishments. As conductors relating to this intelligence we create a mind-body connection in the basic conducting patterns, expressive gestures, and mixed meter patterns we share with our ensembles. The observation of other conductors, and the imitation of both effective and affective musically generating movements are associated with bodily-kinesthetic intelligence.

- **Interpersonal Intelligence** involves working cooperatively in a group through effective, clear, and specific verbal/nonverbal communication with sensitivity to other's moods, temperaments, and feelings. This perhaps is one of the most significant intelligences for student musicians as it is concerned with the capacity to understand the intentions, motivations, and desires of other people, empowering individuals to work effectively with others. Musically they must be sensitive to others, creating a harmonious interaction. The give and take between individuals and the group when dealing with balance, blend, and intonation is evidenced through this interpersonal intelligence. Individual students develop an awareness that complements the sensitivity of the section and full ensemble. When dealing with musical style, expression, phrasing, and dynamics, they must be aware of the subtleties of nuance and inflection through their voice and instrument. Another critical component is working in sectional rehearsals to develop cooperative learning skills. Through collaboration and consensus students develop interpretation, style, and characteristic performance attributes as a cohesive section and ensemble. Principal players and section leaders must be sensitive to others by understanding group processes and developing organizational and management skills. Interpersonal intelligence skills allow students to develop and strengthen their musicianship through performance in ensembles.

- *Intrapersonal Intelligence* is the language of introspection and awareness of internal aspects of self. This includes awareness of one's own feelings, intuitions, and thinking processes. The recognition and control of our thinking as we perform specific tasks, and the employment of this realization to control what we are doing is termed metacognition. Our instrumental teaching techniques deal with concept formation, especially when presenting tone quality, phrasing, and expressive elements. Students become sensitive to their thought and thinking processes and they are consumed as individual members of an ensemble, along with their awareness of section and full ensemble. As their intrapersonal intelligence develops, their intensity and energy of musical thought matures. The development of a spontaneous reaction to keys, chords, harmonic content, style, and rhythm patterns occurs through intrapersonal intelligence. Students gain the means to express their inner feelings and emotions, and become uninhibited as they discover their musical personality. Musical expression is a natural extension of the development of intrapersonal intelligence. However, the key is for the teacher to exhibit this intelligence in order for students to understand and utilize it as well.

- **Visual/Spatial Intelligence** is the language of shapes, images, patterns, designs, color, textures, pictures, and visual symbols. This "inner seeing" involves active imagination, pretending, visual thinking, keen observation, framing mental images and graphic representations, recognizing relationships of patterns and objects, and acknowledging a sense of the "whole." As instrumental teachers, we often refer to the images and beauty of tone quality, balance, blend, and playing in tune as we teach students. The variations of dynamic colors and diverse chord qualities are enhanced through guided visualization. Images and metaphors connect the bits and pieces of musical performance through the mind's eye and the mind's ear.

A meaningful and value-filled band program is comprised of student musicians who understand, appreciate, and are sensitive to each other in our musical world of communication and expression. I believe Gardner's Multiple Intelligences are critical in the development of musicianship and significantly contribute to the students' total educational process. Instrumental music is unlike any other subject or discipline as it effectively spans the entire universe of both cognition and learning. With this, we recognize the depth of a musician, and the demand is likewise on the conductor.

THE CONDUCTOR'S RESPONSIBILITY

A conductor's personal musical depth is critical to the success of the ensemble. As a conductor, your thinking, feeling, and musical expectations are all based upon your musical upbringing and experiences. When we were in elementary school and decided to choose an instrument, we never realized this was no small undertaking. We accepted the demands while shaping our discipline in becoming a musician. A world of solitude greeted us as we practiced endlessly day after day. Through this solitude, our minds were totally immersed in deep thought and analysis while shaping our musical skills.

We then chose to teach music, and quickly realized that there were no shortcuts or college classes that could fill any musical voids. Musical depth comes from years of study, practice, reading, teaching, and simply being immersed in music. Musical depth begins with our early studies as an instrumentalist and continues to expand throughout the years. The anonymous quote is appropriate at this point . . . "*Music gives back what it receives.*" Only when we musically mature with our instrument—having developed a disciplined, musical mind—can we open the door for beautiful music making with students.

Every band director experiences fear and nervousness when he or she first stands before an ensemble . . . a little intimidating. It's not easy to collect our musical thoughts and to then extend them through teaching to our students. Our early fears and nervousness of standing before an ensemble are significant experiences in the shaping of a musical mind.

There are no shortcuts, only the persistence of achieving what our dream was when we first began the study of music. The many years and hours of practice we experienced shaped our musical minds with patience determined by musical imagination. We must strive for musical entrainment, discussed more in chapter 2—a process of joining with the feelings conveyed in the music and projecting this feeling with ensemble members. Perhaps one might almost have an experience of feeling a connection with the composer or performer by sharing emotions and feelings conveyed in the music, either through its creation or through the performance.

Ultimately, the ensemble will naturally sense the feeling that a conductor has within. It is this energy of thoughtful expression that is given to the players. Musicians can sense this connection immediately. If it becomes imitated, contrived, or other, the conductor is a detriment to the ensemble's music-making potential.

This secluded discipline is the major difference between directors and student instrumentalists. You cannot shape your students' musical minds through trivial music. Practice materials, methods, and worthy literature are an absolute necessity in becoming a creative director. Any abbreviation of such materials simply creates a weakness in musical growth.

The exercises presented in the remainder of this book will give you tested and proven techniques for ensuring a fully immersed, involved, and truly successful ensemble. The concepts and teaching techniques that appear here are carefully designed and extensively "field tested." The success that one achieves with this system is a result of connected learning, orchestrated immersion, relaxed alertness, and active processing.

CHAPTER 2.

DESIGNING
EFFECTIVE REHEARSALS

A successful ensemble begins with the conductor, and the first step in designing effective rehearsals is knowing one's overarching goals for the ensemble. Notable composer Alfred Reed had this to say on the topic in an article in the *Canadian Winds Journal* (2003):

> What so obviously must be true to anyone with ears to hear what can be done when music (especially "band" music), is taken seriously in all of its technical as well as artistic aspects at any level of performance, not just Grade VI, by someone who apart from being a conductor is also a musician: one who speaks the language, hears what is behind the physical sounds, and knows how to achieve what he wants to achieve in his performances.

Tied to this larger vision of the whole, the rehearsal period and thoughtful teaching must address key issues: *What is expected of students in the band program? What are students expected to know and be able to do through the study of instrumental music?* These statements have far-reaching implications; take them into consideration when designing a band program of excellence and academic rigor.

Many factors can impede the musical growth of an ensemble. First and foremost is the rehearsal itself. Frequently a rehearsal will become disjointed when the conductor has to stop and re-teach fundamentals. As I taught my students, my emphasis and direction was always to make certain that everyone in the ensemble was at the same level of skill and musical understanding . . . that I had everyone on the "same page." An example of inefficient teaching would be having a weak clarinet section, a strong trumpet section, and a mediocre low brass section. The ensemble's growth is seriously hampered until these inconsistencies are addressed.

The director is responsible for teaching a "musical performance vocabulary" that is applicable to all levels of literature. If a student has any type of weakness in their performance vocabulary, serious problems will develop within the ensemble. All students participating in an instrumental program should ideally demonstrate the highest levels of musical literacy and be able to function through the lifelong learning experience of instrumental music as participants, consumers, and advocates.

The ensemble experience allows the band student to become *actively involved in a decision making process* that ultimately determines the band's quality and excellence. Each participant must be responsible for tuning, balance, blend, rhythm, dynamics, and phrasing. If the director assumes the responsibility in making all musical decisions and denies students the opportunity to develop *their own* critical listening and thinking skills, students become *passive participants waiting to be told what to do.* Throughout the rehearsal, the director must instruct and guide the students through the process of making musical decisions relative to performance demands, challenging individuals to produce to their potential and beyond. Musical understanding is expanded considerably when the individual is placed in a section setting and experiences how his or her decisions impact the final performance. Noted neurologist Dr. Frank Wilson states *in Mind, Muscle and Music Bulletin #4* (Dept. of Neurology, Kaiser-Permanente Medical Center):

> Your training in music must from the very beginning deliberately guide you toward the goal of making your own independent judgments about the quality of your playing. There is a serious threat to your growth if this does not occur, because if someone with greater knowledge must always approve your interpretation, your music ultimately can only be imitative. If this happens, you've missed the boat.

Students must have opportunities to become musically independent.

Likewise, the conductor must be fully immersed in the rehearsal. Ensemble potential and growth is directly impacted by the conductor's actions and decisions, even in rehearsal. Many directors keep their eyes absorbed by the score throughout rehearsal; they are conducting only the notes of the score, and thus are waiting for mistakes. Instead of being proactive and feeling the beauty of the music, they establish a reactionary stance and limit ensemble expression. It is obvious their attention is not focused to the music being made.

In contrast, observe a seasoned conductor with his/her head held high, shaping the music being produced, with only a brief glimpse of the score. The experienced conductor is immersed in the music as he or she spontaneously shapes the contours and beauty of the music being produced. A conductor is similar to a sculptor . . . the sculptor sees the beauty of what is to be created in a block of stone, while the conductor sees the whole of beauty the composer notated on paper. They both shape the beauty of their creations. The creative director conducts the music and not the notes—both in rehearsal and in performance.

Questioning Traditional Rehearsal Techniques

We all have seen a "bit and pieces" rehearsal in many of our observations. In 1992, a survey by Blocher, Greenwood, and Shellahamer presented some interesting observations on teaching behaviors by middle and high school band directors. They found that directors were always getting ready for the next performance. Their rehearsal time was consumed with error detection, endless repetition, and dictated interpretation. They reported, "Band directors were reluctant to trying new approaches to traditional rehearsal practices out of fear that the performance products of their bands will suffer." In other words, these directors failed to question some of our traditional methods, with the usual reply, "Well, we always did it this way." The words of Winston Churchill are significant here: *"Men occasionally stumble over the truth, but most of them pick themselves up and hurry off as if nothing ever happened."*

My word of advice, from experience, is simply to disregard the voices of "convention" and instead listen and learn from the master conductors and teachers . . . never fear to make changes from the conventional approaches.

Throughout my years as a musician and teacher, I made it a point to observe our notable teacher/conductors. I collected hours and hours of cassette tapes of these most notable conductors and composers as they worked with instrumental students. I analyzed these tapes and, through them, gained a deeper understanding of music and the design of an effective rehearsal. The most notable aspect was how these "masters" developed a rehearsal with techniques that flowed through the lyricism of a beautiful composition: adagio, accelerando, ritard, allegro, development, recapitulation, and molto expressivo, to name a few. Such lyrical teaching techniques always captivated and consumed the student's attention with improved performance, resulting in musically efficient rehearsals void of wasted notes or words!

Above all, it is critical to ensure that students understand their roles as part of a totality. The German poet Friedrich Hölderlin wrote: "If man does not find the time for looking at the whole he will stumble again and again. He can only see small things without any context." He further states, "Man must learn to see things as a whole. Then everything will be good and beautiful!" (From "*The Drama of Modern Mankind – According to Thoughts of Friedrich Hölderlin*").

DESIGNING A REHEARSAL

The design of a rehearsal is critical in determining ensemble success. The blueprint includes the timing and pace of musical details to be resolved (teaching techniques) with clear expectations of student responsibilities. Determining what students will know and be able to do by the end of a rehearsal is critical to ensemble growth and development. Teaching and rehearsing is based on the ensemble's mastery of musical fundamentals and the connections drawn to all performance literature. The consistency of the rehearsal template is critical to ensemble development and maturity.

The overall pattern of a rehearsal must be carefully designed. Every director has his or her unique approach and sequence for a rehearsal, and every ensemble is different, determined in large part by the director's teaching style, knowledge, and experience. Therefore, attempting to duplicate or copy another director's rehearsal pattern usually ends with failure. I frequently emphasize to directors to be a creative director—one who shapes a rehearsal period that will create effective musical learning and understanding within his or her specific ensemble.

Efficiency is another characteristic of a creative director's rehearsal design. We must be aware of how many times we have taught something. An efficient director needs only to teach a music fundamental once. A creative director never consumes time with mindless repetition—because mindless repetition is never required if one is using effective teaching techniques. If there are weaknesses in their performance skills, revisit your instructional techniques and process.

In fashioning a more meaningful rehearsal period, consider what has been learned in the study of learning behavior and the psychology of memory. Psychologist Peter Russell, in his publication *The Brain Book*, states that when we are involved in learning, there are four main periods of highest recall: 1) the beginning, 2) the end, 3) activities that are linked to the beginning, and 4) things that are outstanding.

My own conducting experiences agree with Russell. Memory at the beginning and end of a rehearsal are near perfect. Learning falls off rapidly after the first ten minutes and then increases significantly near the end. To overcome this rapid fall off, directors must link the expected musical results (balance, intonation, articulation, rhythm patterns, etc.) from literature to be rehearsed within the warm-up in the first ten minutes. Such a warm-up significantly improves student performance and understanding of what is expected through the entire rehearsal.

As a director, I held high priorities for scale knowledge. The beginning of every rehearsal had some form of what I call the Grand Master Scale, either in major or minor scale form. (The Grand Master Scale is a term I've coined to describe *one* scale exercise that includes *all* major scales.) Following the scale warm-up process was some series of articulation patterns taken from the literature to be rehearsed and applied to a variation of the Grand Master Scale. As all instruments were at room temperature at this point, tuning would now be in order. The tuning process began with the principal tuba sounding an F concert, followed by principal players tuning from the lower pitched instruments to the highest (piccolo). (See chapter 8 for more on tuning.) As "straight line" tuning was in place with principal players, section players then tuned to their section leader. Once full ensemble tuning was in place, various chord qualities were played in all keys to establish a consistent pitch center, balance, blend, and ensemble sonority. Literature would follow the outlined warm-up process.

Importance of the Warm-Up

The warm-up process is as important as the literature to be prepared. This is the time when mental and physical readiness is established. Psychologist Peter Russell states in *The Brain Book*, "A warm-up effect is especially noticeable in learning where retention is enhanced if a person has performed a similar task immediately beforehand." (p. 89)

Some band programs consistently use the same scale, chorale, or other pattern in every warm-up. The result is a chorale tempo that is "etched in stone" and void of musicianship. In fact, I recall having adjudicated two bands from one school, and each played the same warm-up and chorale with the same metronomic tempo. Neither of the bands played in tune and failed to project any type of phrase direction, or other musically expressive understanding . . . they simply played as a sterile exercise. Such analytical techniques limit musical freedom and purpose, and are disjointed from their intended outcomes during rehearsal and performance.

Infusing Variety

Students become quite bored from the monotony of a rehearsal that follows identical or habitual patterns each day, and learning is decreased. Playing some form of a Bb major scale and not experiencing any of the remaining fourteen scales is a typical example of rehearsal monotony. Still, some amount of repetition is necessary to develop good patterns or habits, because there are both positive and negative habits. Positive habits have a direct connection to what is to be rehearsed or performed, and negative habits have no meaning or connections to performance, only consuming time with no purpose. In *Psychology of Learning and Motivation* author Gordon Bower states,

> When a person is presented with a sensory signal that is repeated with monotonous regularity, his response to it gradually diminishes until it becomes undetectable. This process is habituation. Habituation is a mechanism which keeps the brain from being bothered by continuous unimportant signals. (p. 186)

A carefully designed warm-up authenticates the meaning of the rehearsal by fundamentally preparing the learners for the literature to be rehearsed.

ESTABLISHING MENTAL AND PHYSICAL READINESS: THE WARM-UP

If the first ten minutes of rehearsal are the most important for learning, then we must warm up in that time with musical fundamentals that will be consistently expected in all literature. Therefore, warm-ups must include exercises focusing on tone quality, balance, blend, and intonation—elements required when performing every composition. I choose these because these elements of tone quality place all emphasis upon listening, as music is a listening art, and to be most effective, rehearsals must elevate listening to the highest levels of focus and concentration.

To further boost listening skills and ensure more total student immersion, I do not use musical notation, chorales, or other when shaping ensemble tone quality, balance, blend, and intonation. When exercising listening skills, I discovered many years ago that notation significantly *reduces* improvement. Without notation, students' attention and concentration is directed to shaping ensemble tone quality, balance, blend, and intonation. A musical director must carefully describe what students are listening to, and what they are listening for, thus, ensuring that they know what to do with what they hear. Musical decision making in action..

There are several reasons to consider warming up without notation:

Not using notation allows students to expand and exercise their listening skills. Basic music fundamentals such as tone quality, balance, blend, intonation, articulation, dynamics, key tonality, melodic line, harmonic color, and rhythm patterns are just a few important areas that require keen listening skills. These skills need to be exercised for improvement. Notation will detract a student's mind and focus.

Reading notation "turns ears off." As notable scholar, musician, and conductor David Whitwell states in an unpublished collection titled *"Essays on the Origin of Western Music,"* "Music is for the ear, not the eye! Once the eye is eliminated, the ear comes into play." Researcher Edwin Gordon states in his publication, *Learning Sequences in Music*, "The ear must be taught before the eye, if the eye is to take meaning from the printed page of notation." These are powerful statements for directors to consider when warming up their ensembles.

Moreover, notation does not guarantee control over concentration, thinking, or focus throughout an entire exercise or composition. If an ensemble is playing a notated chorale or other, a student can briefly drop out and not be noticed. Without notation, the students' thinking must be focused on the task 100% of the time. If not, the student becomes lost and they become quite uncomfortable. Notation can be a "security blanket" for a warm-up process.

The most critical and significant reason for no musical notation is to make students active participants in making musical decisions with ensemble tone quality and performance. They base their decisions on what they hear. It is the quality of each student's musical decisions that determine the quality and excellence of the entire ensemble. Their musical decisions are the result of applying what they are taught. Again I say: if there are weaknesses in their performance skills, the instructional process and techniques must be questioned and changed.

Exercise 2.1. Teaching from the Circle of 4ths

Teaching musical decision-making begins with teaching students the Circle of 4ths, rather than giving musical notation. I often refer to the Circle of 4ths as *"Everything you wanted to know about music."* I use a handout (see Appendix A), which provides a simple line of pitches based on the interval of the 4th. This sheet may be used in exercising every type of music fundamental, including scale patterns, articulation, chord quality, dynamics, chord progressions, tone quality, balance, blend, intonation, and rhythm patterns, to name a few. The variations are endless and are determined by the director's "creative" mind.

In using the Circle of 4ths instead of notation in my warm-ups, I direct students to play mid-range notes, nothing high or nothing low, using each note of the line of pitches provided on the sheet. They decide what mid-range note they will play. This decision is the beginning of the student's musical decision-making process. Moreover, following the line of pitches is an introduction to all scales/keys and removes the conventional "one scale at a time" approach, which has little to do in shaping a "musical mind" . . . a musician's mind must spontaneously respond to all keys, chord qualities, etc. This triggers a more intense level of thinking, as they have no musical notation to assist with their decision.

You can duplicate the Circle of 4ths sheet (Appendix A) for each student in your ensemble. Use it to instruct students about instrument transpositions, and indicate which note they will begin playing in the line of pitches, in their daily warm-up.

(Please refer to *Student Supplement Book 1* and *Book 2* for unlimited variations of scales, chord qualities, rhythm patterns, and dynamics.)

MORE THOUGHTS ON REMOVING THE NOTATION

You may notice that I removed the notation from the Circle of 4ths sheet. By removing notation, the student immediately connects with pitch names and not notation. Without fail, this simple change elevates thinking and response, and removing notation expands and exercises listening skills. We now can focus listening and playing toward tone quality, balance, blend, intonation, articulation, dynamics, key tonality, melodic line harmonic color, or rhythm patterns. Recall David Whitwell's words: "Music is for the ear, not the eye! Once the eye is eliminated, the ear comes into play."

Another important awareness is that notation does not guarantee any control over concentration, thinking, or focus retention throughout an entire exercise or composition. Without notation, students become active participants in making musical decisions with ensemble tone quality and performance. Too often, students wait to be told what to do by their director; without notation, they decide what to do themselves.

Last, and most important, reading letter symbols establish a communication system common to all instruments. This is the difference of saying "G#" has greater meaning to all students than saying "valves 2 and 3," which relate only to trumpet, French horn, and euphonium.

Your band will progress significantly if you remove notation from your warm-up process. This places listening as the priority, and there is no better way to elevate listening skills. Your rehearsal priorities should be based on eliminating the weaknesses of your ensemble. For example, if your ensemble has articulation problems, then you would emphasize various articulation patterns using the Grand Master Scale, always emphasizing all keys and not only F, Bb, and Eb. If dynamics are an issue, simply play various chord qualities stressing crescendo, decrescendo. (See the appendix for exercises that will help you improve your ensemble's sonority and tonality.)

Above all, in designing your rehearsals, don't waste time searching for a "formula," because no formula will ever cater to *your* ensemble's specific strengths and weaknesses. You are the Creative Director and it is your responsibility to shape and design a rehearsal that helps your ensemble achieve the results you anticipate.

CHAPTER 3.

ENTRAINMENT: THE INVISIBLE COMMUNICATION SYSTEM

Another priority for ensemble development is establishing internal ensemble pulse. I refer to this as "entrainment." Entrainment is readily evident in small ensembles such as trios, quartets, or quintets; they are so rhythmically entrained that conductors are not required. A principal player simply gives a preparatory beat, and the music begins to flow, moving smoothly through transitions, tempo changes, phrasing, dynamics, and a myriad of musical possibilities. **In contrast, traditional thinking is that such entrainment is not necessary in a large ensemble, because setting the pulse is the conductor's job. But I disagree.** Such sensitivity and focus—entrainment—should be a part of *every* large ensemble.

What is most intriguing for many nonmusicians is that this type of small ensemble has an "invisible communication system" that connects the minds of its players. Is this mysterious happening something that others cannot experience? Is it that all players are focused to a point that intensity and energy of "thought" are sensed within the players?

Yes! Let us consider this "invisible communication system," which psychologists refer to *entrainment*. Entrainment is a principle of physics and is defined as the synchronization of two or more rhythmic cycles. The Dutch scientist Christian Huygens in 1665 discovered, while working on the design of the pendulum clock, that when he placed two of them side by side on a wall and swung the pendulums at different rates, they would eventually end up swinging at the same rate. Another example of entrainment occurs with tuning forks. When a tuning fork produces a frequency of 440 Hz and is brought into the vicinity of another tuning fork, the second tuning fork will begin to oscillate at 440 Hz. The first tuning fork has entrained the second, or caused it to resonate.

Entrainment is seldom spoken about in our music training institutions, nor is it addressed through rehearsal techniques. Barry Green discusses entrainment in his

2003 GIA Publication, *The Mastery of Music: Ten Pathways to True Artistry*. Barry Green stated,

> When musicians entrain, they merge and synchronize their actions. These synchronized actions in turn have the potential to reach and entrain the audience as well. And when that happens, as the final crash is heard or last long note fades at the end of a piece, the audience is one, as you can tell from the stunned silence—and the thunderous applause. (p. 24)

The entrainment process is readily evident in music, in several forms: rhythmic entrainment, melodic entrainment, dynamic entrainment, and perhaps most important, performer/audience entrainment. When the music is joined with the listener's feelings—that is, that the listener is stirred by the music—that is full entrainment. The conductor has connected the composer's intention with the listener, through the ensemble's performance. Musical entrainment is the process of joining feelings conveyed in the music, sensing the feeling of commonality with it, and then sharing it with others.

Renowned holistic physician Dr. Andrew Weil states on his Web site,

> An intriguing aspect of the sound of music is entrainment—things vibrating in proximity to each other tend to synchronize their frequencies as they come closer together. The rhythm of music can entrain you...as you're listening to music notice how your body moves in response to it.

A study from the University of Salzburg found that musicians who play in sync are aligning their cognition. The study showed that brain waves became more synchronized as the group played. This study, published in a *BMC Neuroscience Journal*, suggests things people do together, or interpersonally coordinated actions, are preceded and accompanied by brain wave coordination. Of course, this is exactly what happens when playing music in a small or large ensemble. (More information can be found at: www.biomedcentral.com/bmcneurosci/.)

In my early years as a student at Syracuse University School of Music, my friends and I would sit in the lounge and freely improvise two-part inventions, or, if there were three or four of us, we would improvise trios and quartets. Other music students were amazed, and some believed we had memorized all the Bach two-part inventions. Now, knowing what I know, this was a wonderful example of musical entrainment . . . we were so immersed in what we were creating, we could spontaneously respond to every subtle nuance and inflection of the other player. It was much like having "one mind" that made beautiful music. This free-form expression became an important part of my teaching techniques as I realized how powerful this was in the development of a musical mind.

Another example of entrainment is that of a jazz quartet, quintet, or other. The "invisible communication system" is quite apparent in this small ensemble. The musicians are totally aware and connected to time, tempo, style, and harmonic and melodic changes as they spontaneously create a wide range of jazz styles and moods. Another occurrence of "entrainment" within a jazz group is when each musician alternates playing four-measure phrases, and as a group, will sense and feel exactly four measures of time or silence, and they are so fully entrained that they will enter precisely together after this measured space of time or silence—without a conductor.

Establishing entrainment in our ensemble begins with aligning internal pulse. By unifying the thoughtful energy of the conductor with that of the ensemble, the musical results are elevated to an artistic level. Entrainment is the most effective way of extending and infusing concentration within the entire ensemble. This is another extension of developing and enhancing the musical mind. Establishing internal ensemble pulse is the first step in developing full entrainment in your ensemble.

Ensemble, by definition, requires "entrainment." The meaning of the word "ensemble" is far more than "a group of musicians playing together." There are three aspects of the word *ensemble*: (1) the individual player, (2) the section player, and (3) how the individual and section contribute to the "whole" ensemble, resulting in the superior musical qualities of an organization. The conductor should perceive the ensemble as one instrument, but still must place considerable emphasis on how each student's mind functions as an individual, as a section member, and as part of the entire ensemble.

That is why we teach our students to *listen*. The quality of listening exercised when playing as a section determines the overall quality of the ensemble. Students control the musical quality of the organization through how they have been taught to listen . . . what are they listening to, what are they listening for, and what do they do when they hear it? If one individual is not attuned to the specifics of section listening and how it contributes to the total ensemble, there is no overall ensemble quality and sonority suffers. Moreover, excessive rehearsal time is wasted trying to achieve ensemble balance, blend, and intonation.

In listening to and adjudicating ensembles, it is obvious when many of the members in the ensemble hold different perceptions. The ensemble is not unified, resulting in a lack of clarity, style, and characteristic performance. It is not that students failed to prepare their parts. The reason for problems that arise during a performance are fundamentally grounded in the lack of awareness about the important unified thought processes involved when playing in an ensemble. Creating ensemble means aligning the thought processes of the individuals involved so that they are thinking as a unit, both within their sections and within the ensemble as a whole.

The awareness *of* "ensemble" and the immersion *in* "ensemble" is a fundamental component that a conductor must convey in rehearsals, in preparing literature, and ultimately culminating in concert performances. This requires developing rehearsal techniques that *align the timed thought processes so that everyone precisely perceives the musical expectation together, as one person and not varied individuals throughout the group.*

We first must look at where the problem originates from . . . the issue is invisible and is located in the mind. The graphic illustration below demonstrates such a condition.

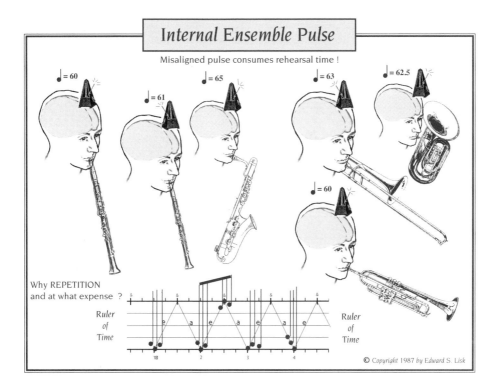

The metronomes indicate the slight variations of tempo and pulse within each individual. The ruler of time illustrates the slight imperfections that occur before, on, or after the beat/pulse. The musical results are poor entrances, releases, and rhythmic imperfection. The performance lacks clarity and definition. This becomes apparent when the director uses percussion to establish a pulse/beat or an electronic metronome, while insisting students either follow "me" or the percussive beat. Thus, enter the world of "repetition" in attempts to align pulse and reaction time to notation. I can assure you, this does not solve the problem.

The following graphic illustrates an aligned internal pulse for precision.

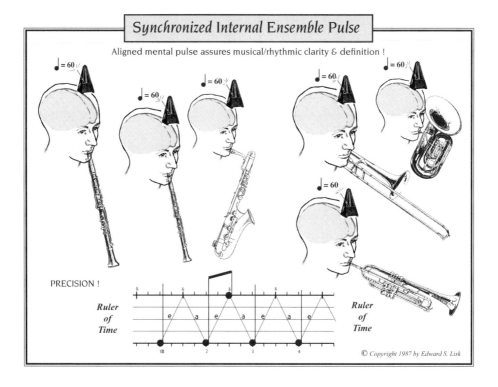

Synchronized Internal Ensemble Pulse

Aligned mental pulse assures musical/rhythmic clarity & definition !

PRECISION !

Ruler of Time

Ruler of Time

© Copyright 1987 by Edward S. Lisk

Once the ensemble's "internal metronomes" are synchronized, as in this graphic, rhythmic precision is in place, thus reducing time consumed with unproductive repetition. Tremendous amounts of time are wasted when using percussion or electronic metronomes to align pulse. Instructional techniques must focus on the root of the problem: accuracy of the internally perceived and experienced pulse.

Aligning pulse and tempo are the highest priority for any ensemble. If pulse and tempo are not perceived with precision, the results will be less than expected, with poor entrances, releases, and the lack of rhythmic precision (as in Internal Ensemble Pulse graphic), among other issues. While I have not observed or read of any rehearsal or teaching techniques that specifically address and exercise internal pulse other than following the tap of a metronome, snare drum, or an amplified tempo device. Internal pulse needs to be exercised just as any other fundamental for playing an instrument. At the elementary level, young students are taught to respond to a foot tap. The problem with a foot tap is that the student can vary the speed or tempo to accommodate any difficult passage. I don't believe there is any connection with thinking in tempo and the foot tap. We already have a built-in metronome, and that is our pulse or heart beat. It's a steady beat (quarter = 60+) and all we have to do is to recognize and apply this to our teaching of time.

With beginner students, I introduce a very simple exercise that immediately makes an important connection with a tempo and pulse by encouraging them to think in time. This process creates musical precision through entrainment. It teaches the students about metacognition: *to be aware of their thinking as they perform specific tasks and then use this awareness to control what they are doing.* Once the students participate in this exercise, you can speak about internal pulse and its consistency and inconsistency. This alerts you and your students to where entrance or rhythmic errors occur. The students must feel and experience a consistent pulse in a mind/body connection that controls the musical action.

This exercise is the first experience in conditioning the mind toward error-free musical decisions—such as making the correct entrance after several beats, measures or rests of silence. This important discipline of duration exercise is not a part of our regular instructional process . . . directors lose confidence in the students' timed thinking through extended measures of silence. Thus, the director is required to "cue" the player or section to assure a correct entrance. A student develops self-confidence knowing his or her internal pulse is correct and connected to all ensemble members. It is not about "following" others; it's being confident that they are correct and aligned in tempo with others. It establishes and expands the student's musical mind and solidifies their musical decisions with accuracy.

Exercising internal ensemble pulse requires consistent rehearsal and lesson time along with director patience. It cannot be assumed that it will develop naturally through repetition. (In addition, I detail internal ensemble pulse in my text, *The Creative Director: Conductor, Teacher, Leader* on pp. 35–39.)

Here is an internal pulse exercise that will quickly improve and entrain your ensemble's rhythmic and performance skills.

Exercise 3.1. Aligning Ensemble Pulse

This can be presented to an individual, small group or full ensemble. The first step is to have the students count out loud from 1 to 8 at a slow tempo, approximately one beat per second or quarter = 58–62. As they count, ask them to listen for the silence between beats or numbers. The space of silence must be consistent. This is a departure from conventional methods, as conventional methods emphasize the sound of the beat (metronome, voice, or drum) for practice and not the silence between beats. When an ensemble rushes or slows down, it is not that they are not following the conductor; it is the space of silence between beats that is changing. If the ensemble begins to rush, the space of silence is becoming smaller. If the ensemble begins to slow down, the space of silence is becoming larger. Simply making the students aware of the silence between beats immediately changes their perception of time keeping. Rushing or slowing down no longer becomes an issue.

As you begin developing an internal pulse with your ensemble, do not use a metronome, snare drum, or other. You will notice that the counting is from 1 to 8, and not 2, 3, or 4 beats. This is an important change in perception and breaks the habit of counting in 2/4, 3/4, and 4/4 time. It represents a departure from the early pages of so many beginning method books that have students playing whole notes followed by whole rests, only counting from 1 to 4, while tapping their foot. Counting from 1 to 4 restricts cognition to one measure at a time and not the duration of the entire exercise. If the exercise is eight measures long with four beats per measure, we need teaching methods to develop and sustain timed thinking for thirty-two seconds (4 X 8) and not four seconds per measure. Counting from 1 to 8 extends the mind of the student into the duration of two measures and not one. This is a departure from the four-beat playing and what I often call a "huff-puff" performance. Moreover, this technique establishes what I often refer to as the Discipline of Duration, a concept that controls and extends the duration of awareness and time through all experiences of extended musical demand, such as the length of a composition.

Teaching students to count from 1 to 8 will lead to more consistent performance results that flow evenly; otherwise, their concentration is only conditioned for 2, 3, or 4 beats or seconds. Why is this important? In the beginning stages, a student struggles as he or she tries to play an instrument while tapping a foot, blowing air into the instrument, and remembering fingerings. The result can be quite discouraging, as this traditional instructional process simply is never questioned. Students are frequently criticized for lack of attention, concentration, or practice. But in this case, students are not at fault; it is the system that has failed to increase timed concentration as it only disciplined the mind to 4 seconds. This very simple counting exercise overcomes such discrepancies. This process is a very important ingredient in shaping the student's musical mind.

Exercise 3.2.

Ask your students to count from 1 to 8 and hold your hands outstretched with palms up. Inform students that they are to count aloud when your palms are up and silently count when you turn your palms down. Do this several times, as this is the essential component of this exercise, and it requires every student to concentrate and maintain a consistent beat or pulse. Hold your palms down for four to five silent counts and then turn your palms up and listen for the accuracy and clarity when the students count aloud.

The silent counts happen randomly. They can begin on counts 2, 3, 4, 5, 6, 7, or 8. It is important to have students count at least from 1 to 8 to establish a steady tempo before turning your palms down. Extend the silent counting to 3, 4, 5, 6 beats/seconds or longer to exercise and expand timed concentration. Continue this process even though a few may make mistakes. If they begin to rush the counting, simply remind them about the space of silence between the beats. The objective is to exercise accurately timed thinking and responding. After the ensemble begins to develop this capacity, you will realize how quickly pulse can be aligned. Moreover, you have 100% of the students on task, thinking alike in tempo . . . you have complete control of their timed thinking process by developing the discipline of duration.

This exercise requires the director to silently count along with the students in the same tempo. This establishes a tempo connection (entrainment) between students and conductor as both internalize the matched pulse. The beauty of establishing this internal pulse will be realized immediately in rehearsals. As a conductor, you will not have to worry about the students following your beat . . . the ensemble pulse is already established and you are able to focus all attention to shaping the music. A word of caution: If the director does not silently count with the students, the exercise will be a waste of time; remember we should perceive the ensemble (conductor and players) as one instrument. This connection between student and director is important. It is "ensemble."

Periodically, challenge your students to see how long they can focus their concentration in tempo silently. By using a tempo of a quarter = 60, focused attention can be anywhere from 3 seconds to 8 seconds or longer. The objective of this process is to exercise and extend the power of internal timed concentration for the duration of a composition. The ultimate goal is the application and transfer of the alignment of ensemble pulse from practice, warm-up, and rehearsal through the fruition of musical literature in concert. This intellectual and internal exercise elevates focused ensemble concentration and easily resolves mistakes in rehearsal or performance. This realization of the mind-body connection to musicianship heightens awareness and musicality of the ensemble as a whole. Thus, creating intensity within the entire ensemble . . . the "magic" of music!

A word of caution when holding your palms down as students silently count to themselves; the longer or extended number of beats for silence (10, 11, 12, or more), the higher the demand for focused concentration. It will take several sessions with this exercise to increase silent timed concentration for 7, 8, or more seconds. Be patient and within a short period, students will be able to silently count beyond the 8 seconds and well into at least 15 or more seconds. This exercise is a prelude into building timed musical concentration and shaping the musical mind.

Exercise 3.3. Making a Mind-Body Connection

Aligning internal ensemble pulse is an excellent process by which to address a mind-body connection. For many years, we have read and heard about the mind-body connection that occurs in playing an instrument. This exercise develops a physical response to notes and rhythm patterns by connecting the notation to students' minds and training them to respond to a particular beat. Review the outlined process below before presenting to your students.

Count from 1 to 8. Turn palms down and up to review the timed focused concentration through silence.

Challenge 1. Instruct students to clap on beats 2, 5, 6, and 8. We are connecting the mind to the body, training it to dictate a handclap on a specific count.

After the students clap the exercise, show them the musical example below. Please note: The counting is not two measures of four beats to a bar; counting to 8 is important, as the exercise is shaping timed concentration to 8 seconds.

Challenge 2. Repeat the counting and have students clap on beats 3, 5, and 8.

After the students clap the exercise, show them the musical example below.

Challenge 3. Instruct students to clap on the "&" of 2, beat 5, and the "&" of 7.

After the students clap the exercise, show them the musical example below.

Challenge 4. Instruct students to clap on the "e-&-a" of 2, the "&" of 3, and beat 6. This is more complicated and requires mental and physical coordination.

After the students clap the exercise, show them the musical example below.

The illustration above gives you an idea of what is being exercised. Create your own rhythm exercises to elevate this very important awareness for reaction and response. Show the students that if their mind is not "connected" to the silence/rests, what follows will always be an error . . . the rests must be active through the timed thinking process in order to create the notated rhythm pattern. Remember: Your exercises should have students counting from 1 to 8, in order to retain focus and concentration.

I suggest that when a new rhythm pattern is introduced in the student's method book, first have the student speak the subdivided pattern, followed by clapping the pattern as they speak the subdivision. Finally, have them play the pattern on their instrument. It is important to emphasize and silently internalize the counting in their minds as they play the pattern on their instruments. Remind the students that the instrument has no intelligence . . . intelligence must flow into and through the instrument for the expected results. We are developing this mind body connection for error-free performance.

Exercise 3.4. Apply Chord Qualities

Follow this exercise with the entire ensemble playing sustained chord patterns (major, minor, dominant, etc.) using the Circle of 4ths. Inform the ensemble to sustain, as they silently counted with the above exercise, up to a given number: 5, 6, 7, or

8. Assign various numbers for duration such as sustain for 5 and rest 3. When you introduce measured silence such as "rest 3, rest 4," or other duration of silence, students should begin with silently speaking the word "rest" in place of the first beat. Try this: Instruct student to "sustain 6, rest 4," then tell them, *"Now let me hear what will be going on in your mind . . . speak."* The students then speak 1, 2, 3, 4, 5, 6, rest 2, 3, 4. Listen for accuracy of pulse and unified speaking, as the next pitch in the Circle will begin precisely on beat 1. Apply these duration exercises with chord qualities and play through the Circle of 4ths.

This simple counting exercise eliminates poor entrances and releases. You can refer to an entrance as being the left side of a note and a release as being the right side of a note. This adds another dimension to your teaching techniques. The right side of a note is sound being lifted off the canvas of silence. (More on this in coming pages.) When this discipline of duration or internal ensemble pulse is in place, students have complete control of entrances and releases. Moreover, students realize immediately where and why mistakes occur when the ensemble's internal pulse is not aligned and precise. I always point out with students the origin of a "mistake." The origin of the mistake occurs in their minds.

Exercise 3.5. Breath Support

I cannot stress enough the importance of establishing an internal pulse as outlined. Consistent breath support is required for this exercise. As the student sustains a pitch for a given number of beats, they must also determine how much air they are going to use to get to the end of the note . . . thus, the name, "discipline of duration." How often have you heard a beginning flute student play a note that consumed all the air, resulting in breathing after every note (huff-puff)? This simple counting exercise is a means to eliminate such a situation. Ask your students to blow air through a drinking straw as they silently count from 1 to 5. Follow this with having them blow air from 1 to 7, 8, and longer. The silent counting automatically controls the volume of air being used. This can be applied with any instrument. You and your students will be amazed with the improvement that results from such an exercise.

It is important to recognize where poor entrances and releases come from: the director! In workshops, I demonstrate by aligning the ensemble's internal pulse through breathing in tempo with the preparatory beat and using the very smallest move with my baton. The result is a perfect (or flawless) entrance . . . this is the result of aligned internal ensemble pulse with ensemble and conductor as one being! The biggest mistake I believe we make in rehearsals is to teach students to "follow me."

Once this becomes embedded within an ensemble, frustration follows. The tempo will fluctuate in rehearsals and performances. The statement does not exercise the student's response or reaction to an internalized or felt pulse, but only to "follow" the beat. The band continues to slow down or attempts to "catch up" to the beat, and continues to make poor entrances. What must be taught is that the pulse/beat is "now" and not before (trying to follow), or after (trying to catch up).

The preceding chapters established a foundation for this new dimension in teaching, thinking, practicing, and playing an instrument. We now enter into the mysterious world of musical expression. The next four chapters include thoughts and concepts to help you shape artistic expression and add a new dimension to your rehearsal and teaching techniques.

CHAPTER 4.

TEACHING MUSICAL ARTISTRY AND EXPRESSION

What determines artistic performance? How are artistic decisions made and are they necessary for musical meaning to occur? These important questions need to be asked both at the very beginning of a student's musical learning, and when a student arrives at a point in their musical studies to determine their success as they pursue a professional career. As musicians and conductors, we are immersed in the fine art of detail, encompassing a multitude of subtle embellishments that are impossible to notate and extremely difficult to teach. To teach artistry requires a teacher who understands and is able to demonstrate on his or her instrument the spontaneity of artistic expression and not something contrived, which we so often hear. As Pablo Casals states,

> The written note is like a strait jacket, whereas music, like life itself, is constant movement, continuous spontaneity, free from any restrictions... There are so many excellent instrumentalists who are completely obsessed by the printed note, whereas it has a very limited power to express what the music actually means. (p. 70)

My composer friend Stephen Melillo once said this in a workshop we were doing together in Pennsylvania: *"How can a caged man teach you to fly?"* If you are not musically expressive as an instrumentalist and conductor, you are not able to understand or teach artistic expression. You are the proverbial caged man. Of course, becoming "uncaged" doesn't happen overnight. Musical artistry evolves and consumes countless hours of practice to discover and experience the smallest musical entity. We can easily hear the difference between sterile and artistic performance with ensembles and individual players. In observing our "legends," I considered the number of hours and years it took them to get to their artistic side of music making. It took many years to have confidence in the artistic decisions that made them so unique. There are no shortcuts for developing artistic expression.

There are four statements I make when teaching for musical artistry. The statements enhance artistic considerations and musical decisions.

1. Music is sound moving in and out of silence.
2. Don't play square notes.   --
3. Notes remain trivial until they are animated with feeling and spirit.
4. If you can't say it, you can't play it.

1. The first statement, *"Music is sound moving in and out of silence,"* plays a significant role in how music is perceived. It also dissolves the boundaries of notation. Too often, music becomes a "paint by number" exercise, as musicians fear going outside the boundaries of notation. For example, they prepare a piece for adjudication, and play the notes correctly, but do not dare to go beyond the unadorned musical notation. But music is an art and not a "paint by number" exercise. If we teach students to imagine an artist's brush "lifting off into the white of canvas," the sound disappears into infinity or the white of the canvas, dissolving the boundaries. Applying this statement to musical sound and considering our "canvas" to be "silence," we discover the "right side" of a note as we "lift the sound off into silence" without a contrived end, simply decaying into the quiet. Silence is indicated by different rest values. If we interpret the rest value and acknowledge the natural decay of sound, the size and value of the rest is abbreviated.

    I have seen several publications try to illustrate this natural decay by drawing a box with a slightly tapered right side. This type of design focuses the mind to something other than artistic thought. Another technique that attempts to address the right side of note is referred to as a "score order release." (Score order release means that the flutes (highest) will be the first to release, followed by all mid to low range instruments releasing as they appear in score order.) I believe such a statement removes the player from hearing and being a part of the total sound while placing importance on the individual player. Do string instruments stop notes? Listen to a string player play a half note and as they lift the bow off the string, you will hear the natural decay of the string and body of the instrument, or the "right side" of the note. By not teaching the right side of a note, the students miss the beauty of resonance and decay . . . or the artist's brush lifting the color off into the silence of the white canvas.

2. *Don't play square notes.* Music is sound moving in and out of silence, and "square notes" lack personality and are often uncharacteristic to the style of music being performed. All notes must have "life" and be energized with nuance and inflection (and are lifted off into silence). Moreover, square

notes are much like "painting by number" and not going outside the boundary lines. Consider the natural decay of a note beyond the boundary line. The subtle musical nuances and inflections are impossible to notate . . . this is left up to the player and conductor to interpret. Playing notes and rhythms precisely as they appear produces sterile and uncharacteristic sounds with no meaning attached.

3. *Notes remain trivial until they are animated with feeling and spirit.* This statement is connected to the first two statements about sound into silence and square notes. Music has personality and character. It is alive and must "say something." And it takes a lifetime to experience all of its details, as so beautifully stated in my favorite quote by Pablo Casals, *"We can never exhaust the multiplicity of nuances and subtleties which make the charm of music."* My teacher always told me that musical expression is found behind the notes. There is nothing behind the notes, only you. Your musical imagination, personality, and expressivity create and embellish the charm of music. This is what makes music unique with every musician and conductor.

4. *If you can't say it, you can't play it.* This not only holds true for phrasing and expression, but also for rhythmic articulation. Too often students have problems understanding rhythm patterns because they were never required to speak the pattern. I always taught my students to respond to rhythm patterns by speaking the subdivided pattern. When they clearly speak and articulate the pattern, they simply play what they speak with their instrument. The instrument on its own has no intelligence. This is the "rhythmic intelligence" that must be projected through the instrument. Surprisingly, the student will always play the pattern correctly. Simply stated, *"If you can't say it, you can't play it."* If you can't say it, it's obvious you don't understand it. This is one of the largest gaps that exist in our day-to-day teaching techniques.

Students understand these four powerful statements. They sound simple, but don't let the simplicity of the statements fool you. They hold considerable musical depth and meaning. Most important, they are connected to all concepts and techniques throughout this system of musical learning, and must all be exercised in all keys, using the Circle of 4ths.

Will music expression continue to be a mystery? If we teach the art of music, shouldn't musical expression be rightfully taught? It is obvious that we can discern between mechanical and artistic performance. The misconceptions and discrepancies that continue to occur with musical expression, phrasing, and other interpretive expectations are due to inconsistent preparation of instrumental teachers (as presented by Daniel Levitin in *This Is Your Brain On Music*). When will all universities require future directors to study musical expressivity? If what I write in this publication triggers your interest in finding out about how to teach musical expression, I encourage you to read my publication, *The Intangibles of Musical Performance.* The concepts and methods presented herein provide a new dimension when teaching expression.

Why do we do what we do? It all goes back to our first musical performance when we felt that "chill" when the music connected with our feelings. We entered the music profession to capture more of such moments. This should be what is expected with every ensemble capable of playing expressively and responding spontaneously to the musical statement. Notable psychologists refer to this "chill" as reaching the summit, of reaching self-actualization, or by experiencing flow; as musicians and educators, this is why we do what we do.

CHAPTER 5.

CONNECTING THE NUANCE AND INFLECTIONS OF LANGUAGE WITH MUSIC

There is extensive research substantiating the connection of music to language. John Sloboda, Professor of Psychology at Keele University UK, states in *Exploring the Musical Mind*,

> . . . some of the most important things about music seem to arise from the ways it is different from a language. But language offers a way of thinking about music which is useful and illuminating. (p. 175)

Neuroscientist Aniruddh Patel, Fellow at San Diego's Neurosciences Institute and author of *Music, Language, and the Brain*, provides the first synthesis, arguing that music and language share deep and critical connections, and comparative research provides a powerful way to study the cognitive and neural mechanisms underlying these uniquely human abilities. He states, "Comparing ordinary language to instrumental music forces us to search for the hidden connections that unify obviously different phenomena." John Sloboda further states:

> His perspective claims of music and language have specialized representations (such as pitch intervals in music, and nouns and verbs in language), share a number of basic processing mechanisms, and that the comparative study of music and language provides a powerful way to explore these mechanisms.

Patel discovered the native language spoken by composers was mirrored in the stress and intonation of their music. He found a composer's work is the musical mirror of his or her primary spoken language. Viewing music as a language and recognizing its similarities to our English idiom is enlightening. I do not believe there are any differences in the way the mind perceives the signs and symbols of the English language and those of music. The only difference is the appearance and design of the signs and symbols and how our brain interprets their values and meanings. However, music educators seldom make any connections to how we speak, read, or listen to the English language in regard to music. When rehearsing an ensemble, I frequently will read a program note in a monotone, arrhythmic, and unemotional style for the students as an example of how they may be playing musical phrases. I then read the statement a second time emphasizing words in context with nuance and inflection, changing rhythmic flow and dynamics to create feeling and meaning. This is the purest means to enlighten one's awareness to the energy and direction of a musical phrase. Students immediately realize the expansion and contraction of the melodic line and where commas, periods, or exclamation points fit into the musical statement.

Consider the words about musical expression by Menahem Pressler, one of the world's most distinguished and honoured musicians and teachers, in Barry Green's book *The Mastery of Music*: "The subtle emphasis can be communicated in music, by comparing it to how we speak."

Prosody is the rhythm, stress, and intonation of speech and sometimes referred to as "the melody of language." The word originates from the Greek *prosoidia*, meaning accent, modulation, and all features that characterize speech. Prosody involves the rhythm, length, and tenseness of gestures, mouthing, and facial expressions. When applying the word *prosody* to the rhythmic flow and lyricism of musical phrases and patterns, I discovered our deep emotional expressive center can be accessed, releasing "felt expression" without being mechanically contrived (like so many methods and approaches). Dr. Michael Gazzaniga states in his text, *Human: The Science Behind What Makes Us Unique*, "Prosody is the musical cue of language: melody, meter, rhythm, and timbre. Prosody helps delineate the phrase boundaries"(p. 237). He goes on further to state,

> Like language, music has phrase structure and recursion. You can create an endless variety of musical phrases by putting together different notes and groups of notes. Just as humans are easily able to assemble phrases into an infinite number of meaningful sentences, we are able to structure and process multiple musical phrases. (pp. 237-238)

Everyone possesses the language of expression! Prosody is natural.

How often have you heard young students counting rhythm patterns in a sustained monotone voice? This monotone response began in our first lessons when our teacher asked us to count rhythm patterns. The patterns were usually written on one line of the staff and implied no pitch changes. This unembellished rhythmic monotone response became embedded in our minds and resulted in making musical expression simply by using dynamic changes, crescendos, decrescendos, adding breath marks, and on and on. As one reads text, there is a natural flow of word rhythms and sentences. There are no symbols to indicate any type of inflection with the words. It is the reader or speaker that implies the meaning and expression through the nuance and subtle inflections of words and statements. The monotone flow of words and sentences hampers reading comprehension and the ability to communicate.

The secret, now uncovered, is based in our everyday language and speech. True musical expression must be "connected" or internalized with the musician's inner soul. These feelings project style, interpretation, and musical meaning. We can incorporate all of the signs and symbols represented on the score and still be devoid of true musical beauty. I wonder if Pablo Casals ever believed there was a connection to our English language when he stated, "We can never exhaust the multiplicity of nuances and subtleties which make the charm of music."

When I study or rehearse a score, I see the musical sentence structure, musical questions, musical paragraphs, musical chapters, and musical punctuation marks through the composer's notation. As I read the English language, I see the rhythmic patterns of sentences, the intonation of words, and the dynamic nuance and inflection that create meaning in what I am reading. I strongly encourage you to begin looking at music in this manner. I assure you, musical meaning will take on an entirely new dimension in your teaching and rehearsing.

Our profession seems to divorce any connections between music and the signs and symbols of our English language. Notable Stanford Linguistic professor (emeritus) Dwight Bolinger states,

> . . . neuropsychological research indicates that melodic contours in speech and music may be processed in an overlapping way in the brain. These and other findings suggest that musical and spoken melody are in fact more closely related than has generally been believed.

When guest conducting, I receive outstanding results when I use inflections, nuance, and rhythmic flow of words with students when teaching musical expression. Understanding and musical results are instantaneous . . . the first time!

With so many years in this profession, I'm still amazed at the number of ways clinicians perceive the art of musical expression. We still cling to the "conventional" crescendo that leads to the high point of a phrase and a decrescendo followed by a comma to indicate a breath mark that signifies the end of the phrase. Focus is not placed in the energy of thought that creates a meaningful phrase. The energy of thought is the origin of musical expression. In the English language, this can be likened to how we speak for coherency, comprehension, and meaning. The energy of thought must "point to something," creating forward motion, intensity, and direction. As the notable Robert Shaw stated, "a phrase is departing from, passing through, and arriving at" to create musical meaning. It is inherent that thoughtful energy activates musical movement, thus shaping the direction of a phrase from beginning to end. Too often music is contrived by simply and inaccurately stating, "Make a crescendo." When this misdirection is given, the intended musical outcome and purpose of the phrase is unclear.

Composers indicate tempo markings, dynamics, articulations, changing tempo, and other signs to assist the conductor in arriving at an interpretive conclusion. I find when reading a score for the first time, it is quite easy to discern a correct tempo, understand the meaning and flow of phrases, and arrive at an expressive interpretation. Stylistic elucidation is easy to determine as it is based upon rhythm patterns, melodic direction, and articulation indicated by the composer. Moreover, we have many interpretive options when considering the musical impacts of a composition. What is most important is that the interpretation is sincere to the individual and not an imitation or copy.

I am including a few graphic illustrations from my previous publications to further the connections of "thoughtful energy" in language and musical phrasing. In *Expression in Music* (original copyright 1926 and later published by Rubank, Inc.), author H.A. Vandercook illustrates the importance of accent and emphasis with a sentence. The illustration repeats a sentence five times, each time placing the accent or emphasis on a different word. When reading each line, emphasis is on the word in capital letters. I have taken the liberty of placing a rhythm pattern beside each sentence (not found in the publication). The arrows indicate the rhythmic flow and "thoughtful energy" moving to a point of repose.

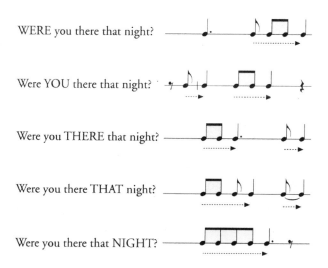

Exercise 5.1. The Energy of Rhythm

Igor Stravinsky stated, "All music is nothing more than a succession of impulses that converge towards a definite point of repose." I refer to it as *"short looks for long."* In other words, short notes are always energized and moving forward, and the long note is the *point of repose or relief of the short note energy moving forward.* The following examples illustrate various rhythm patterns based upon this *natural moving* concept... The important consideration is given to the "long" note; it is always related to the short notes that come before.

It is important to recognize the direction in which the rhythm pattern is moving. As you read the rhythm examples, treat the long note as if you discovered or found someone you were searching for . . . as in "Aha, there you are!" Suspense exists in the short notes searching for relief. Just before the arrival of the long note, experiment with a very slight delay to increase suspense. It is ever so slight, but apparent, creating meaning and interest through the rhythm pattern. The arrows below each pattern indicate the direction or energy of thought, which will always lead to the long note as in resolution, discovery, or the point of repose. The direction or energy of thought releases one's artistic considerations. The life and energy of musical expression is similar to speaking. Your students should practice the following rhythm patterns with their instrument. First use the nonsense syllables (ta, da, etc.) and then have them play the "felt" expression with their instrument.

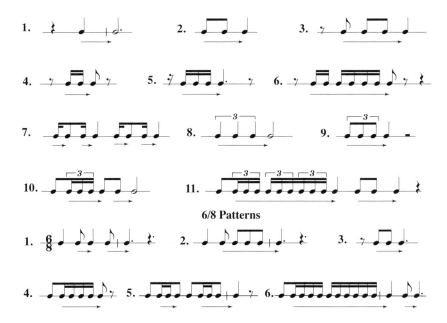

I urge you to check your scores and recognize that all rhythm patterns function in this manner, in this flow of *short looking for long*. If you don't recognize the energy and logical movement of rhythm patterns, your musical interpretation will not project a coherent, meaningful statement as intended by the composer. The vitality and continuity of musical expression cannot exist in any other manner.

My intention is to prompt an added dimension in your musical decisions when preparing a composition for performance. To transform your musicality and that of your ensemble requires meaningful consideration to what truly originates in a musician's mind to form musical conclusions.

CHAPTER 6.

CONNECTING FEELING
TO RHYTHM

A logical sequence for expanding and connecting musical expression to notation is to exercise counting rhythm patterns with subtle nuances and inflections. It is important to repeat Pablo Casals statement, "We can never exhaust the multiplicity of nuances and subtleties which make the charm of music."

Frequently, students are asked to count a rhythm pattern with its subdivision. Usually, the student gives a monotone response with very little voice inflection; it is cold, unresponsive, and suggests that the exercise was musically meaningless for the student. It is at this time when expressive performance should become a part of the instructional process. This is the first opportunity for students to become connected to *meaning* and *value*.

Patience and encouragement are important. The process expands an individual's expressive options through the subtle nuances and inflections of feelings projected through their voice. It is an extremely simple approach to develop musical expression at an early age. A student must have opportunities to exercise their "feeling" just as any other musical skill.

Exercise 6.1. Expression Through Rhythm

The instructional process begins with the student counting any subdivided rhythm pattern of least four measures in length. This step will not feel unusual or difficult for the student; it should be something they are comfortable doing. To create greater value for students, apply the process with rhythm patterns found in their band selections or method books.

Step 1. Count the subdivision in tempo (1 & 2-e-&-a etc.)

Step 2. Change the language of subdivision to the language of expression (non-sense syllables) La, loo, li, di, do, de, ta, ti . . . or whatever syllable feels comfortable. *Do not try to learn a set of unnatural syllables* for this exercise. *Natural* is the key for success. Learning another set of programmed syllables becomes a mechanical repetitive process emphasizing something different from natural expression.

Step 3. Add the subtle nuance and inflection of personal feeling and meaning to the *nonsense syllables* . . . as if making a statement with emotion such as sadness, joy, happiness, profound announcement, etc. Experiment with different inflections, nuance, emphasis, volume, and spoken tempo. The exercise establishes a natural *connection* between mind and felt expression, and eliminates the mystery of musical expression. *The voice utterance projects this connection with the nuance and inflection of felt expression.*

It is important to support and encourage the student to experiment with *feelings* and not hesitate to take the *risk*. Once students feel comfortable speaking patterns with nuance and inflections, then have them play this same expressed *meaning* and *feeling* into their instrument. Create the same nuance and inflection with a comfortable note. Once students experience this process, they have gained entry into the world of artistic expression . . . *This mind/body connection fills the space between contrived and artistic expression!*

Using H.A. Vandercook's earlier example of accent and emphasis with different words, have your students first speak the rhythm pattern (with subtle nuance and inflections), and then play the pattern on their instruments. The musical example is based on the first five notes of a scale.

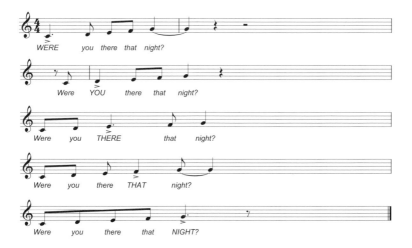

I have included a simple rhythm pattern from Stephen Melillo's statement used in chapter 7 to further exercise the connection of musical nuance and thought with notation. The statement is: "It was a time of turbulence, when seafaring men dared claim the waters of the earth…a time when the crimson blade of treachery, slashed across trusting hearts." As you speak the statement be sensitive to the slight nuances and inflections when speaking.

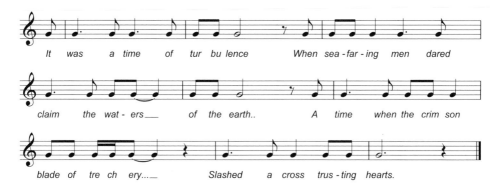

We are creating expressive experiences for students beyond the typical crescendo and decrescendo methods so often used. The student must understand that the instrument has no intelligence, and the intelligence must come from somewhere . . . *intelligence flows into and through the instrument.* Simple! Students immediately connect with this technique and quickly discover the meaning of "feeling" and how easily it becomes a part of their musical performance. It develops focused concentration.

As your students experience this new connection of feeling to rhythm patterns, you now have another method to apply to band literature phrasing and solo performance.

CHAPTER 7.

DEVELOPING AND EXERCISING MUSICAL EXPRESSION

David Levitin's wonderful publication *This Is Your Brain On Music* addresses a frightening condition that exists in our universities today. Dr. Levitin writes,

So much of the research on musical expertise has looked for accomplishment in the wrong place, in the facility of fingers rather than the expressiveness of emotion. I recently asked the dean of one of the top music schools in North America about this paradox. At what point in the curriculum is emotion and expressivity taught? Her answer was that they aren't taught. 'There is so much to cover in the approved curriculum,' she explained, 'repertoire, ensemble, and solo training, sight singing, sight reading, music theory – that there simply isn't time to teach expressivity.' (p. 208)

David Levitin responded with, "So how do we get expressive musicians?" Her answer: "Some of them come in already knowing how to move a listener. Usually they've figured it out themselves somewhere along the line." She further stated, "Occasionally, if there's an exceptional student, there's time during the last part of their last semester to coach them on emotion." Perhaps this is the answer for those unmusical ensembles we frequently hear . . . expression is an afterthought, even at the nation's finest conservatory.

A recent study published in the *Psychology of Music Journal*, vol. 36, "Musical Expression: An Observational Study of Instrumental Study," by Jessika Karlsson and Patrik Juslin, stated the following:

Research has shown that both music students and teachers think that expression is important. Yet, we know little about how expression is taught to students. Such knowledge is needed in order to enhance teaching of expression. The aim of this study was thus to explore the nature of instrumental music teaching in its natural context, with a focus on expression and emotion. Results suggested that the focus of teaching was mainly on technique and on the written score. Lessons were dominated by talk, with the teacher doing most of the talking. Issues concerning expression and emotion were mostly dealt with implicitly rather than explicitly, although some teachers used a variety of strategies to enhance expression. Although there were individual differences among teachers, a common feature was the lack of clear goals, specific tasks, and systematic teaching patterns.

Finally, someone admitted why we have so many unmusical performances today. Musical expression is not taught. Over the period of thirty plus years, I made it a point to attend many clinic presentations dealing with musical expression. Unfortunately, very few ever hit the target regarding the truth and integrity of musical expression. Presentations typically outline the need for score study, analysis of form, rhythm, and phrases. Most presentations dealt with "contrived" phrasing and expression and were not connected to musical meaning, never addressing the internal energy of thought or forward motion of perceived phrases.

One of the most important components of a well-designed instrumental education program is the opportunity for students to exercise "expression" and "feeling." I have not experienced any methods or techniques written for this type of learning. A few publications do make an attempt to address this part of music making, and at the end, the methods and techniques are quite mechanical—meaning, contrived.

Worse, many of our conventional methods and techniques actually condition our students to play without expression, like the sterile and lifeless notation written in a lesson book. As we inform our students to "play with more feeling," it is impossible to bring "life" to the musical notation if the relevant teaching process is not in place. Moreover, I have viewed rehearsals where the director tells a story in an attempt to have students "do something expressive" with the notes. Students cannot do something expressive with the notes if they were never taught how to be expressive with the notes. It seems the many routine attempts to achieve musical feeling fall short of anything meaning filled.

Exercise 7.1. Discovering the Soul of Musical Expression

This exercise truly awakens a student's expressive musicality. When presenting musical expression in my workshops and clinics, I use a statement from notable composer Stephen Melillo, found below, as the first step in this exercise. This is an eye-opening experience and the directors and students immediately "get the message" and understand where feeling and expression must come from. As I continually state, the instrument has no intelligence; intelligence must flow into the instrument. Feeling begins within the individual before anything enters into the instrument . . . feeling must enter and flow through the instrument. So, the question is, how do you exercise feeling and expression? Hopefully this is not accomplished by telling stories about various scenic illustrations, or other nonmusical events.

The first step in this exercise is to have the student read the following statement. It is the same type of exercise as outlined earlier in H.A. Vandercook's publication *Expression in Music,* where he illustrates the importance of accent and emphasis with a sentence.

> It was a time of turbulence . . .
> When sea-faring men dared claim the waters of the earth . . .
> A time when the crimson blade of treachery,
> Slashed across trusting hearts.

As each student reads the statement, you will hear how reserved and inhibited students become when trying to be expressive. The same is true when they play their instruments. Students have difficulty expressing themselves freely as they expect specific teacher-defined directions for correctness. Here, we encounter their fear of risk, which stifles or hinders their expressive potential. This is exactly what occurs when they play musical phrases. They want the teacher to advise them as to where the crescendo, decrescendo, accents, etc. should be. This is as far as they go with musical expression; they don't exercise their own decision making process. This is a significant reason to include expressive learning experiences that guide students in realizing their musical potential.

To relieve some of the anxiety with students, use the Vandercook illustration where he stresses the importance of accent and emphasis with a sentence. Such as . . . *IT was a TIME of turbulence, or, It WAS a time of TURBULENCE!* This will usually remove some of the inhibitions.

Have the students read the statement a second and third time with more exaggeration and dramatic insistence as the statement and words imply. This energized response to the words of this statement is identical to what is projected through the instrument when responding to notation, rhythm patterns, and phrases. This simple exercise unveils the mystery of musical expression, and activates the same neuro-signals (emotional centers) we use for verbal descriptions.

Remember, expression is the interpretation of signs and symbols, coupled with the individual's personality. There is no difference between musical and personal expression; the emotional connections between the individual's spoken word and music notation are identical. Feeling is feeling whether it is through verbal communication, painting, sound, dance, or other. The problem is, many of us have never considered or traced the origins of emotion and its connection to musical or spoken expression. I hope that this publication finally has solved the mystery.

Personal expression is what creates musical interpretation. The differences with interpretation are what make it unique to each individual. Early attempts at practicing this concept will be uncomfortable for students. This is typically a learning experience never before encountered through any of our accepted methods. Be patient and encouraging with this process . . . students will initially perceive this as a risk and feel uncomfortable, as this will be a new endeavor for most. Over time, with patience and support, this significant discovery will bring meaning to students as they realize their full expressive and creative musical potential. And remember: This exercise in expression also applies to the conductor. Be mindful that any reservations while engaged in this process will suppress musical expression.

I found this speaking exercise in personal expression to be an eye-opening encounter for band directors who attend my sessions. They are stunned because this discovery makes so much *musical* sense. Many directors who felt they were attuned to musical expression now uncover a whole new meaning and purpose for themselves and their students. This approach appears in few, if any, other publications, and most directors I've encountered in workshops report that it was not a part of their undergraduate or graduate levels of study. But universally, directors report that their students clearly understand musical expression when this method is implemented into their instructional program.

Exercise 7.2. Dynamics: Reading With True Expression

To emphasize the lack of expressiveness when one is consumed with musical symbols, have the students read the following. It will be quite apparent as to how silly the statement becomes.

The above exercise is presented to make you aware of the difficulty to freely express the statement without being overly consumed with crescendos, accelerando, etc.—and instead focus on making meaningful musical expression. Try this with your students, and you will immediately realize a significant change in the way they play their instruments. Musical phrases are brought to life when they connect them to feelings that exist in their hearts and minds. This is a totally new dimension in teaching the beauty of musical expression and how we deal with the unadorned markings of musical notation!

It was a time of turbulence...

ff ———————————— *ppp*

When sea-faring men dared claim the waters of the earth...

sfz ——————— *fff accel.* ⌢ ——————— *pp*

A time when the crimson blade of treachery,

Molto rubato..............................

slashed across trusting hearts.

rit.............................. ppp

Why Practice Expression

I am a strong believer in the need to "exercise" expression with the same intensity as we exercise skill development. I believe the only reason this part of musicianship is so lacking within our programs is the fact that students and directors feel insecure when attempting to teach musical expression. Moreover, we were not prepared in our undergraduate or graduate studies to understand the truth and integrity of true musical expression. I say this because I have witnessed directors who are embarrassed when I ask them to be expressive while reading a statement or paragraph. They were never made aware that expression with words and sounds comes from the same source within our body. When expressive reading and its application to music is not exercised, words such as *beauty, gentle, touching, sadness, crying, glory, elegance, precious, glisten, love,* and the many descriptors of feeling have very little meaning in our lives. If "feeling" is not exercised in all of music making, it will atrophy. This is the one and only reason we hear bands that are unexpressive. An ensemble needs to develop a personality that shares its musical beauty with the listeners. If not, then it cannot be called music.

THREE NATURAL LAWS OF MUSICAL EXPRESSION

In my publication, *The Intangibles of Musical Performance*, I speak about the *Natural Laws of Musical Expression*. There are only three books that I know of that I believe address the truth and integrity of musical expression. Those books were *Casals and the Art of Interpretation* by David Blum, Donald Barra's *The Dynamic Performance*, and James Jordan's *The Musician's Soul*. As stated earlier, most methods and rehearsal techniques fail to go beyond the mechanical and contrived descriptions. After many years of performance, I arrived at three simple concepts that can account for the thousands and thousands of words attempting to describe musical expression.

1.   Short looks for long.
2.   Low searches for high.
3.   High searches for low.

The word "searches" implies energy, motion, and forward movement looking for a point of repose: *Low searches for high*. *High* is the point of repose. When applying this concept to phrases, determine the low and high note in the phrase. The notes in between create the feeling of energy and motion moving to the high note. The notes in between create the "tension," and the arrival of the high note is the "relief" of the phrase or point of repose. It is important to repeat Robert Shaw's statement, "A phrase is departing from, passing through, and arriving at" to create musical meaning.

Applying this statement to *low searching for high* simply means departing from the low note, passing through the notes in between, and arriving at the high note. When a phrase is perceived in this manner, the subtle nuances and inflections enhance the artistic interpretation. This energy of thought must "point to something," creating forward motion, intensity, and direction. It is inherent that thoughtful energy energizes musical movement, thus shaping the direction of a phrase from beginning to end. Specific details and exercises regarding these simple musical concepts are presented in my recent publication, *The Creative Director: Conductor, Teacher, Leader*, and *The Intangibles of Musical Performance*. I strongly suggest you read these publications to get a better understanding of musical expression and techniques and apply it to your instrumental program.

Below is an illustration of the three concepts *high searches for low, low searches for high* and *short looks for long*.

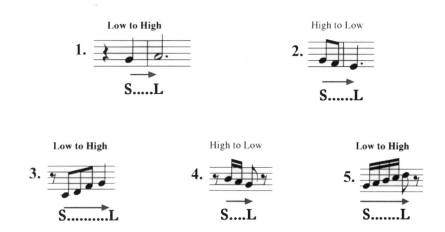

Many of the current texts describing musical expression fail to acknowledge the underlying principles and the importance of the thought process that triggers the movement of an expressive melodic line. Many attempts to create this through some form of markings, dynamics, or other which has very little to do with the spontaneity and integrity of producing an expressive phrase. As David Levitin writes in *This Is Your Brain on Music*, *"So much of the research on musical expertise has looked for accomplishment in the wrong place, in the facility of fingers rather than the expressiveness of emotion."* (p. 208)

<table>
<tr><td> </td></tr>
</table>

Exercise 7.3. Expanding and Contracting Sound: Dynamics

A weakness that prompted Alternative Rehearsal Techniques was dealing with how dynamics, crescendo, and decrescendo are taught. In my early years, adjudicators consistently remarked about the lack of dynamic contrast with my ensemble. As I thought about this, I realized that I did use my left hand to indicate a crescendo or decrescendo . . . this didn't work. I also taught my students to respond to the symbol that indicates a crescendo and decrescendo . . . this didn't work. I was already using the instructional process that I outlined in an earlier chapter regarding an internal ensemble pulse. This was the answer . . . why didn't I think of this sooner? I simply used the numbers from 1 to 8 and explained to the students that "1" would be piano, and "8" would be forte. Simply count from 1 to 8 and with each beat, speak louder just as you would turn the volume control more loudly on a CD player. Reverse the numbers and it would be the same as turning the volume down one beat at a time. This immediately solved the problem of dynamic contrast. Moreover, I no longer had to use my left hand to indicate a crescendo or decrescendo. The students understood what the symbols meant. They responded and applied what they learned. From this point on, I occasionally reviewed the process and I no longer had any adjudicators commenting on the lack of dynamic control.

Dynamic interpretation needs attention when preparing an ensemble for a concert. Dynamics are relative—and the word "relative" too often is not taken into consideration. When dealing with dynamics, directors tend to exaggerate dynamic markings to the extent that piano (p) becomes too soft (at the expense of tone quality) and forte (f) becomes too loud (at the expense of tone quality). Too often adjudicators will stress the need to expand an ensemble's dynamic range. It is at this time I believe the "exaggeration" of dynamics enters into a rehearsal setting.

I developed a very effective exercise when dealing with dynamics and teaching the meaning of "relative." I ask the students to speak the word "1" at a piano level. When they speak "1" piano, I respond with, "If that is piano, what will pianissimo (pp) be?" They speak "1" pianissimo, I then ask, "What will pianississimo (ppp) be?" When asking for pianissimo and pianississimo, their voices quickly become a whisper. It is at this point, I state, "You can't play soft at the expense of tone quality, balance, blend, intonation, or harmonic content."

Tone quality is the priority . . . this is important when speaking dynamics. Students make the change immediately, and tone quality improves significantly. I then use a higher number to indicate a higher dynamic level. I then ask, "Let me hear 5 at forte (f) . . . If that is forte, what will mezzo-forte (mf) be? . . . What will fortissimo (ff) be?" etc. This exercise quickly alerts the students to relative dynamic decisions.

The above dynamic process is also an outgrowth of the earlier technique establishing a consistent internal ensemble pulse by counting from 1 to 8. Using this number system will produce consistent crescendo and decrescendo response. The dynamic counting system I am proposing is far beyond the typical left hand rising to imply a crescendo or moving downward for a decrescendo. By assigning the number "1" as being piano (p), and "8" being a forte (f), the students count aloud and increase volume on each number or beat (same as turning up the volume on a radio). First ask to hear what "1" will sound like by speaking the number as piano (p). Second, ask to hear what "8" will sound like by speaking "8" as forte (f). If you are satisfied with the two dynamic levels, then continue the exercise by asking the students to count from 1 to 8 and remember how the volume increase feels with their voice. This will be the same feeling that will be projected through their instrument. The next step is to have the students play a pitch while silently counting the number of beats assigned to the crescendo. You will hear a very well played crescendo after a couple of times.

The decrescendo exercise is the same only that the numbers are in reverse order (same as turning down the volume on a radio). Students will speak "8" at a forte (f) level and then "1" at a piano (p) level. Follow this by having students count from 8 to 1 in reverse order with the dynamic change with volume. You will hear a very well played decrescendo after a couple of times. This exercise conditions air distribution when increasing or decreasing volume. When the entire ensemble responds in this manner, no longer does the tone color of crescendo or decrescendo change. This method is the only means to establish controlled dynamics and tonal color.

Another approach to demonstrate the consistency of dynamic changes is to show the students what a crescendo "looks like." Simply say that "1" is piano or seated in the chair, and "5" is forte or standing. As they gradually count from 1 to 5, they slowly rise with each beat. Do the same in reverse and reversing the numbers from 5 to 1 will seat the entire ensemble. You will see the uniformity of everyone rising followed by being seated . . . a wonderful visual of dynamics.

When you apply this concept to band literature, ignore beat numbers such as 1, 2, 3, 4. If a "pp" begins on a beat other than "1" and ends with a "ff" on a third beat, for example, simply begin counting from the indicated "pp" as being "1" and continue counting (ignore measure beats) to the "ff." This will give you the total number of beats for the crescendo. An example would be a 9-beat crescendo from 1 to 9 . . . 1 being "pp" and 9 being "ff." If a decrescendo is indicated, apply the same counting system to determine the duration of the decrescendo and simply reverse the numbers (9, 8, 7, 6, etc.).

This dynamic counting system is designed to prepare students to play consistent dynamic changes from either a soft or loud level. The "meaning" of the musical symbol for crescendo or decrescendo becomes a part of their music reading skill. They will respond without having the director inform them that there is a crescendo or decrescendo. Moreover, once your students are prepared in this dynamic response, you will no longer have to "use your left hand" to create a crescendo or decrescendo. Is it necessary for a conductor to indicate "something" that is already written and expected? Is it that we have failed to effectively teach the students to respond to the musical symbol of crescendo and decrescendo? Throughout my travels, I frequently will demonstrate to directors what they can do with their left hand, other than indicating crescendo or decrescendo, when the students effectively respond to such dynamics. No longer does the left hand have to indicate a crescendo or decrescendo. One example is to use your left hand moving in a horizontal direction from right to left, implying the flow and duration of a phrase.

When performing literature that may feature a solo, the dynamic range for the solo must be adjusted. Usually when a "p" or "mp" is indicated for the solo passage, the soloist does not project over the ensemble. More often, the dynamic level and sonority of the ensemble are sacrificed as the students attempt to play extremely soft at the expense of tone quality. It is much more advantageous to ask the soloist to increase the dynamics and project over the full ensemble. Pablo Casals statement supports this dynamic adjustment stating,

> When we see piano (p), the composer means in the range of piano. The range of piano extends all the way to forte (f) and the range of forte extends all the way to piano. One has to follow the line of the music. If it goes up, you have to give more, despite the piano. Otherwise it is something that is not free . . . not what the music intends.

> Musical judgment and decisions are the priority in this case.

CHAPTER 8.

SHAPING ENSEMBLE TONE QUALITY AND SONORITY

What are the musical ingredients that establish an ensemble's full, rich, sonorous tone quality? Establishing ensemble tone quality and sonority is an area that needs considerable attention. It is much more than simply tuning to an electronic device or adhering to all the dynamic markings. It is how a director applies balance, blend, and intonation not in one, two, or three keys, but in all fifteen major keys. As a director, you must establish a process that will exercise the student's listening skills in all fifteen major keys and various chord qualities (major, minor, dominant, diminished, etc.). This procedure tends to be overlooked or not emphasized enough in our preparation to become directors.

The overall sound of your ensemble will be unique from all others. I refer to many bands as "sound-a-like" bands. Why do so many bands fail to arrive and establish an ensemble sound identity? Before an ensemble sound identity can be established, an aural image must exist in the director's mind and ear. Many publications have addressed this difficult area of band performance. Perhaps listing a few of our band "legends" and their prominent ensembles with their unique ensemble tone quality will assist you in establishing an aural image: Eastman Wind Ensemble (Fennell), U.S. Marine Band "President's Own" (Bourgeois, Foley, Colburn), U.S. Air Force Band (Gabriel), University of Michigan Symphonic Band (Revelli), University of Illinois Symphonic Band (Begian), New England Conservatory Wind Ensemble (Battisti), Northwestern University Symphonic Band (Paynter), Ohio State University Concert Band (McGinnis), to name just a few. I have been fortunate to observe all of these ensembles in rehearsal and concert. It was obvious each conductor had a unique "sound" etched in his or her ear and mind. Young directors should not be discouraged; this unique sound and aural image is shaped through many years of experience.

SEATING ARRANGEMENTS

Before an ensemble's tone quality can be improved, we must first look at the seating arrangement that is being used. There are many variations. My seating priorities are focused upon the placement of principal players and their proximity to each other. This is crucial, as the principal players establish a "pitch center" that must remain constant throughout an entire rehearsal or concert. The next priority is in the placing of woodwind choir, brass choir, and percussion. If the choir is not set up with consideration for principal players and supporting "colors" (2nd and 3rd players, alto, tenor, and bass voices), serious balance and blend issues will result. As an example, it is not a good idea to have the trumpets on one side of the ensemble and trombones on the opposite side. This creates a situation where it is impossible for the brass section to sound balanced and blended, and intonation becomes inconsistent.

Another significant contributor to ensemble tone quality is the number of players per part. A word of caution: place fewer students on the first parts, followed by second and third parts. A clarinet section (or trumpet section) would be two 1st clarinets, three 2nd clarinets, and four 3rd clarinets. This kind of part distribution will give you the best balance for your ensemble. Another issue that creates balance problems is the fact the better players are assigned to a higher seat while the lesser skilled players are at the lower end of the section. This kind of part distribution prohibits a full, rich, sonorous ensemble sound, as the balance issue is near impossible to resolve.

Below is a graphic of the seating plan I used with my high school wind ensemble and I frequently use in my travels.

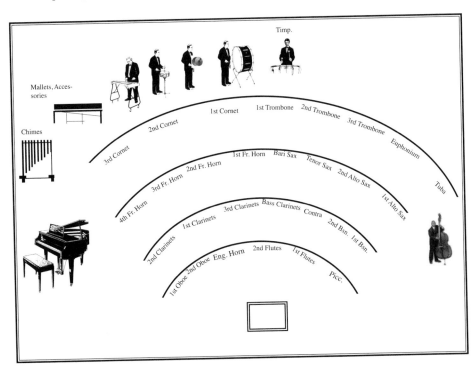

SHAPING ENSEMBLE TONE QUALITY

Step 1. Dynamic Balance

The first area to address in shaping an ensemble's tone quality is dynamic balance. We frequently see dynamic markings in our musical scores that may indicate all instruments are to play "ff" or other dynamic levels. If this is observed, a significantly out-of-balance sound will be the result. Considering the science of sound, higher pitched frequencies travel much faster than lower pitched frequencies. Understanding the speed of high, mid, and low frequencies requires volume adjustment with the upper range instruments while increasing mid and lower range instruments. If not, a very bright and edgy sound will destroy the warmth and texture of an instrumental ensemble. Beautiful depth and warmth of an ensemble simply requires increasing volume levels of mid, low range instruments, and lessening the volume for high range instruments.

Step 2. Blend

The second area of importance after balance is blend. Blend in an ensemble means playing with characteristic tone quality. Poor tone quality will not blend with good tone quality. A beautiful tone is the result of proper embouchure, breath support, posture, and equipment (instrument, mouthpiece, reed, etc.). The student must first hear himself/herself playing with a beautiful tone. If not, the quality of sound will not sound appealing to the listener. As the saying goes, "Beauty lies within the eye of the beholder."

Step 3. Intonation

Finally, after balance and blend have been addressed, intonation logically follows. Intonation cannot be placed before balance or blend. An out-of-balance pitch cannot be tuned properly with a target pitch (target pitch means the appointed section leader or principal player). Poor tone quality will not blend with a section or target pitch. Therefore, balance and blend must be solidified before intonation.

There are a few misconceptions about balance, blend, and intonation. Frequently, directors attempt to teach balance, blend, or intonation in isolation, without connecting all three concepts *to* tone quality. I always stress that our top priority is tone quality, and within tone quality, we have balance, blend, and intonation. Tone quality, balance, blend, and intonation cannot be divorced from each other.

TONE QUALITY

Below are a few more examples for balance, blend, and intonation, all of which place the responsibility of musical decision-making on the student. Let's revisit:

1. You can't play loud at the expense of tone quality, balance, blend, intonation, or harmonic content.
2. You can't play soft at the expense of tone quality, balance, blend, intonation, or harmonic content.
3. You can't play short at the expense of tone quality, balance, blend, intonation, or harmonic content.

With such statements, everything is based upon tone quality. Tone quality is a result of what the word "beauty" means to a student. If students don't hear themselves playing with a beautiful tone quality, all the descriptors have very little meaning. Tone quality is built on breath support, embouchure, posture, and equipment. With that in place, the word "beauty" determines the result. Simply reminding students about these statements immediately triggers a positive response . . . you will hear the difference.

Couple the above three decision-making procedures with the four areas I listed earlier in Chapter 4 dealing with artistic considerations.

1. "Music is sound moving in and out of silence."
2. "Don't play square notes."
3. "Notes remain trivial until they are animated with feeling and spirit."
4. "If you can't say it, you can't play it."

When conducting an ensemble, my musical decisions determine the spontaneous interpretation and the shaping of music being produced. Listening is first directed to the ensemble's tone quality based upon balance, blend, and intonation. It is the conductor's responsibility to change it to what he or she holds as the aural image of a particular ensemble. As with any ensemble, tone quality is the top priority. This is the first response from an audience, whether they understand tone quality or not. If the sound is not what they anticipated, appreciation is minimal. At this point, I listen to the sounds being produced vertically relative to harmonic content and structure. My musical decisions are based upon what I will do with the melodic contour, or sound being produced horizontally based on harmonic content (vertical sound). Such decision-making supports the fact that musical interpretation is unique with every conductor. No two performances will be alike.

Exercise 8.1. Balance, Blend, and Intonation

Below you will find a very simple process that can be taught to your students. It is so simple, yet the results are overwhelming. The process places all responsibilities on the student and the musical decisions they are making . . . the students are held accountable for balance, blend and, intonation of THEIR ensemble.

	Issue	Action	Resolution
Balance	You are overblowing your section or ensemble	Adjust the volume and lose your identity	This musical decision controls ensemble **Balance**
Blend	If you still hear yourself and you made the adjustment with **Balance**, you are playing with poor tone quality	Poor tone quality will not **Blend** with your section or ensemble, and a physical/mechanical adjustment is needed	Check embouchure, breath support, posture, and equipment (reed, mouthpiece) and lose your identity
Intonation	If you still hear yourself and you made the adjustment with **Balance** and **Blend**, you are not playing in tune	In order to play in tune, you must adjust the length of your instrument	Make an adjustment to the tubing/barrel (shorten or lengthen) or an adjustment to the mouthpiece (in or out)

THE PROBLEM WITH TUNING

I have written several articles and chapters regarding "The Mysterious World of In-Tune Playing" (*Teaching Music Through Performance in Band*, Volume 5, GIA publication). My tuning procedures are designed to tune the entire ensemble in every key and not via one or two notes. I discovered many years ago that to teach an ensemble to play in-tune in all keys is not difficult. Tuning is a simple process and a strobe is unnecessary. I have witnessed many tuning variations attempted by bands, and these attempts were void of any understanding of the science of sound. The many processes currently in use are riddled with inefficiencies and never achieve the desired outcome (this includes university bands). When we hear an out-of-tune band, it is obvious that the instructional system for listening and tuning is flawed and needs to be changed.

Early in my musical career (as a clarinetist), I was taught to listen to determine if a note was sharp or flat. This was quite confusing for me, as my teacher's directions were difficult to understand. This was a heavy burden through these early years, finally relieved when I attended summer classes at Eastman School of Music to study clarinet and to take a class with notable scholar and expert on the science of sound, Everett Gates. It was Everett Gates who finally put all the pieces of the tuning puzzle together and from that point on, teaching students how to play in tune was no longer a mystery.

My first suspicion of the traditional tuning approach came in my first year of teaching when I attempted to teach intonation. I did exactly what I observed with so many band programs: students tuned to the strobe . . . this indicated that they were now in-tune. We then began rehearsing literature. I quickly realized that the precision of the strobe did not make my band play in tune. What do I do now? I continued my observations of area bands to see whether there were any "secrets." Unfortunately, there were none. I continued my search to establish a tuning system that would assure my ensembles that *all* notes, not just one Bb tuning note, would be in tune.

At this point in my early teaching career I changed my tuning procedures with my high school band. I switched from tuning to Bb concert to F concert. What a dramatic difference it made with ensemble tone quality, sonority, and ease of tuning. No longer did I have that typical bright, edgy sound that usually ended as being A-443 or higher, relative to a Bb concert. F concert tuning is a very comfortable note for students to tune, also alleviating embouchure pressure (no more pinched 3rd space C for trumpets).

I discovered that F concert was an extremely comfortable note for all instruments. Yes, this is a trouble note for the Bb clarinet, as it is called a "throat tone." I can still recall in the early 1960s how clarinets were tuned to Bb concert. When listening to a concert back in those days, we would hear clarinets out of tune in the throat register. The fact remains: the clarinet is an instrument that is designed to the interval of the 12th. It was University of Illinois band director Mark Hindsley who initiated the tuning of throat tones first before any other pitch. Mark Hindsley understood the science of tuning with long and short tube notes. He used Eb concert and F concert to tune his clarinet section, which was known to be the best in-tune clarinet section of any university ensemble.

When attending concerts it is obvious when a band tunes to an F concert versus a Bb concert. The F concert band has a darker, fuller, and more sonorous sound. A Bb tuned band has a bright and edgy sound because of pitch sharpness and balance issues.

If you are using a Bb concert to tune your band, I am hopeful that you will consider investigating a tuning process based on F concert. By tuning to a Bb concert, instruments were being tuned with long tube and short tube notes. The science of sound dictates that this creates a major conflict. Unfortunately, many directors do not acknowledge this discrepancy. A clarinet at Bb concert is referred to as a "full tube" note. Couple this with a flute playing Bb, which is a short tube note. Short tube notes tend to be sharp, and long tube notes tend to be flat. This is a major issue with the clarinet and flute sections. Band directors often wonder why their flute section (and piccolo) sound flat. A French horn section tuning to a Bb concert plays their first space F. If the French horn tunes to F concert, they use 3rd space C. They can check both sides (Bb and F) of the horn using this pitch along with checking the C below the staff.

The only instrument in the band that Bb concert is a good tuning note for is the Eb alto sax. Tuning the alto sax to an F concert places the tuning note on fourth-line D, which is not a good note because of its sharpness on that particular instrument. To resolve this issue, simply teach your student how to compensate for the D relative to the G (Bb concert). The alto sax can use the G to tune beatless against an F concert.

Some directors take issue with me regarding the F concert tuning. Their response is, "What are you going to do with the alto sax players?" My response is, "Does this mean you will sacrifice all other instruments for the saxophone section, or will you teach the saxophone section how to compensate for the sharpness?"

Another situation that happens frequently is tuning the entire ensemble to a clarinet sounding a Bb concert. I always smile when this happens because this is an absolute scientific impossibility to expect a tuba to tune up to a clarinet. Simply stated, science dictates that higher pitched instruments must be in tune first with lower pitched instruments (as with the harmonics of the overtone series). Thus, for intonation consistency, an ensemble should tune from the bottom up, or tuba. This applies, of course, to school bands. It is particularly important for young bands; professional organizations do not tune in this manner, as their members are experienced players with keen listening skills.

Before bringing this section to closure, I am aware of the issues that so many refer to as good notes and bad notes on brass and woodwind instruments. It is important to understand the cent deviations of your particular instrument. Once you have trained your ear to listen for in-tuneness through scales and chords in all keys, the cent deviations are no longer necessary as this focuses your mind to something other than the music you are playing.

My priority was to design a tuning system that would span the entire range of an ensemble in all keys and chord qualities. This tuning system had to be in context with the timbre of instruments and not "foreign to the ear" as an electronic device or sine wave.

I strongly discourage the use of an electronically produced pitch (sine wave) for tuning because it is out of context for wind players. An electronic pitch is a foreign sound. Tuning should always be done with instruments so the produced pitch relates to section and ensemble tone quality in rehearsals and concerts. The ear must be conditioned to hear the various instrument timbres and not foreign produced sounds.

Unfortunately, tuning has become extremely complex for students and directors. There are tuning procedures that are promoted that are impossible to achieve when playing in an ensemble. I urge extreme caution in the process you apply with your students. Simplicity is the answer.

TUNING BY THE LAW OF SOUND: OVERTONE SERIES

To achieve the highest level of listening skills, you and your ensemble must have an understanding of the overtone series. When using the overtone series for tuning, it is simple to eliminate any intonation problems an ensemble may be experiencing. Awareness of the overtone series helps students produce a beatless pitch perfectly in tune by relying on their ears as they listen for the unisons, octaves, fifths, and fourths. (Reference my current publication, *The Creative Director: Conductor, Teacher, Leader*, for additional information regarding overtone tuning and graphic illustrations.)

Overtone Series for Tuning

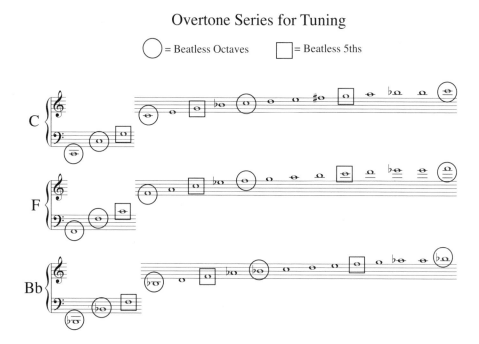

Understanding the overtone series and applying the system to ensemble tuning should be our top priority in developing superior ensemble tone quality and sonority. For so many years, our profession did not recognize the "science of sound" and never considered overtone tuning. In Wilmer Bartholomew's well-known publication *Acoustics of Music,* he states:

> Tone quality depends upon the number of overtones and the way the energy is distributed among them . . . . If a set of ten or more tuning forks, mounted on resonator boxes, and comprising a fundamental tone and its harmonic partials and if the fundamental is sounded alone, a sweet dull sound will result. Then if one after the other of the partials are added, the tone will become more and more full, rich, sonorous, and "living." (pp. 13, 20)

Notable composer Robert Jager states: "Composers utilize the overtone series as part of their harmonic language. If the music is performed out of tune or misunderstood, then the overtone series is destroyed, and the composer's intentions are not fulfilled." Perhaps with Jager's statement, a higher priority should be placed upon overtone tuning.

Dealing with balance issues, Robert Jourdain states in *Music, The Brain, and Ecstasy*:

> Played softly, a low frequency tone must have ten times the energy of a midrange tone to sound as loud and almost a hundred times the energy at higher levels. Our ears are most sensitive to high tones, which require only a fraction of the energy as loud as midrange tones. (p. 42)

Robert Jourdain's statement makes a great deal of sense when considering balance, blend, and intonation. It is easy to understand the serious balance problem that occurs when a *forte* or *fortissimo* is written in all parts. Dynamics must be adjusted to maintain balance between high and low pitches.

When tuning an ensemble, one must also understand that pitch is relative and is not stationary. Pitch varies throughout a concert. This is why I question many methods that teach + and – cent deviations. If pitch were stationary and not affected by temperature, embouchure, breath support, and instrument brand, tuning with + and – cent deviations would be acceptable. My professional performance background dictates my stance regarding pitch as being relative and changing throughout a concert. It is virtually impossible to believe that a pitch center will be stable and consistent. The issue is how are the students taught to listen and adjust to these subtle variations. Students must consistently be listening and making musical decisions to eliminate any beat deviations that will disturb tone quality and sonority. The "ear" must be conditioned and exercised to adjust every pitch in every key and remain consistent throughout an entire concert.

Another weakness with traditional tuning is when a director stops the ensemble to tune one note in a composition. Attempting to make such a correction is totally out of context with the notes that are a part of a chord that may precede and follow the intonation error. To authenticate the process/concepts of tuning and intonation, we must move beyond isolation of specific notes and/or chords and into the context "of" the music. We must use instructional techniques that rely on the laws of sound: what is the student listening to, what is it that they are listening for, and what do they do with it after they hear it?

TUNING AN INSTRUMENT

The process I use is connected to and is an outgrowth of the three steps for listening and shaping ensemble tone quality as outlined in the illustration in exercise 8.1.

The tuning of an instrument is an extremely simple process. Students must understand "straight line" or "beatless" tuning (aligning misplaced frequencies). The tuning line is the only straight line in music. If this pitch line is jagged, the ensemble suffers. Students must have a "target" to tune to. Never ask a group of students to play better in tune if you have not identified a "target" player. The "target" is the principal player or section leader. This individual will always be correct. Any pitch discrepancy with the principal player should be addressed in a lesson setting and checked with a strobe to maintain an F concert relative to A-440. When the principal players in each section tune to the fundamental pitch as the "law of sound" (tuba), there is an aural target rather than a visual one (a strobe picture). When two or more players try to play in tune without identifying a target player, it is nearly impossible to resolve the pitch discrepancies.

As students tune to their principal player, they listen for "beats" or misplaced frequencies. If the beats are rapid relative to the principal player, they must make a move either in or out with their tuning slide, barrel, or mouthpiece (woodwind instruments). If the beats slow down, they are making the correct move. If they speed up, make a move in the opposite direction. When two or more pitches sound as one and there are no pulsations, a "straight line" is in place, and they are perfectly in tune. As instrumentalists *"lose their identity,"* they are unable to detect any individual, and the sound is perfectly balanced, blended, and in tune within the section.

Tuning is a three-part process in the mind. First, playing in tune begins as an individual decision, when each player matches the target pitch (principal player) to make a "straight line" of sound. Second, the individual's in-tune pitch must be per-fectly matched with the section when the section plays a straight-line unison with the section leader (individuals *lose their identity*). When the capacity for section listening and decision making is developed and employed by all members, individual contri-butions to the full ensemble's in-tuneness and overall tone quality is realized.

You may have noticed that with all of these steps and procedures, I again used the phrase *"lose their identity."* Too often, a section will play the same pitch and the varia-tions of tone quality, balance, and blend are easily noted. If there are nine trumpets and they all play the same pitch, I do not want to hear nine variations of the same pitch; I want to hear one uniform pitch (straight line) played by nine players. We are dealing with precision for balance, blend, and intonation based upon tone qual-ity. Therefore, students must lose their identity within a section. When this occurs, inform the students that they are playing perfectly in tune. It is important to use such positive reinforcement, as it develops confidence. Too many conductors neglect to congratulate in-tune playing and instead focus only on resolving errors. Conse-quently, the ensemble never achieves satisfaction or confidence when playing their instrument.

TUNING WITH THE CIRCLE OF 4THS

I guarantee immediate improvement with your ensemble if you implement these simple concepts and procedures outlined, all of which are referenced in my previ-ous publications. They go beyond the traditional approaches and are based upon the science of sound. To arrive at and establish the consistent ensemble tone quality and sonority, simply pass out the Circle of 4ths sheet and exercise listening in all keys.

FULL-ENSEMBLE TUNING

The graphic below illustrates three tuning exercises for full ensemble. The exercises are used after principal players tune, followed by section tuning as outlined above. It is best to dictate each pitch while giving the students time to make their adjustments. As the ensemble plays through the Circle of 4ths (necessary to tune ALL keys and pitches), remind the students of their responsibilities if they hear themselves. Their musical decisions determine the quality or your ensemble . . . allow them time to develop their ear and musical decisions. You will find several variations in my publi-cation, *The Creative Director: Conductor, Teacher, Leader.*

Exercise 8.2. Full-Ensemble Tuning

FULL ENSEMBLE TUNING EXERCISES (Using Circle of 4ths)
Exercise Tuning in All Keys

Group 1: F, Bb, Eb, Ab, etc.
Group 2: C, F, Bb, Eb, etc.
Group 3: C, F, Bb, Eb, etc.
Group 4: F, Bb, Eb, Ab, etc.

Group 1: F, G, F, - Bb, C, Bb, etc. (do-re-do)
Group 2: C, D, C, - F, G, F, etc. (do-re-do)
Group 3: C, D, C, - F, G, F, etc. (do-re-do)
Group 4: F, G, F, - Bb, C, Bb, etc. (do-re-do)

Group 1: F, G, F, - Bb, A, Bb, etc. (do-ti-do)
Group 2: C, B, C, - F, G, F, etc. (do-ti-do)
Group 3: C, B, C, - F, G, F, etc. (do-ti-do)
Group 4: F, G, F, - Bb, A, Bb, etc. (do-ti-do)

To achieve a full, rich, sonorous ensemble sound, Group 4 instruments provide the fundamental pitch for all others to listen for and become a part of. Group 1 cannot "pass" (volume) the sound of Group 4 and Groups 2 and 3 are to play "inside" the sound of Group 4.

After a few weeks of tuning your ensemble as outlined, I assure that you will be amazed at how well your ensemble will sound . . . the science of sound dictates the result.

SCALES: DEVELOPING ENSEMBLE SKILLS

An ensemble can have strengths and weaknesses. The greatest weakness is the variation of technical skills. Some sections have outstanding players and other sections may have mediocre players. The outstanding players easily mask the mediocre players but still hamper the selection of literature you may choose to study and rehearse. In my early years, I attempted to get every student "on the same page" when it came to their technical skill level. After years of various method books, etude studies, and other means to elevate the ensemble's skill level, I realized there was one extremely important exercise that I failed to emphasize: scales.

My students were just like many students who did not enjoy practicing scales. I looked at how scales were used in various ensembles: Scales are used for many reasons other than music making. Scales are used as tests, chair placement, and for passing or failing grades, to name a few. We as directors are the guilty individuals who shape this negative attitude for scales. After much thought, I realized the answer was that students did not believe that playing a scale was "music making." Who would ever think that playing one scale was not music?

I was uncomfortable having students play scales one at a time. To me, this wasn't music, and playing one scale at a time had very little connection to any of the literature we were rehearsing. I became aware that when a scale was played, the student only had to control their thinking and tempo for approximately three measures at most. The first note was usually a quarter note and the top note was a quarter and the last note usually a whole note. These long notes were much like a "security blanket" for students. When they arrived at the last whole note, their mind became dormant. I realized how flawed this scale system was, yet it is still in use today. Music is not one key. It is our responsibility to shape the students' musical minds. They must respond, error free, to notation through their performance vocabulary. Therefore, it is important to establish new worth and value for scale knowledge.

The Problem With Scale Teaching

Throughout my travels, I spend a considerable amount of time speaking about scales. Scales are in fact one of the biggest weak points in many teaching approaches. My big question is, why do so many refer to only twelve scales? I wonder what three scales do not exist and what about the relative minor scales. As my good friend and composer Stephen Melillo stated, "Mahler wrote in Gb and Eric Korngold wrote in F#...which one of these composers was wrong?"

I was taught that there were fifteen major scales . . . because there are actually fifteen key signatures. Every student that I taught learned to play fifteen major scales and their relative minor scales. I believe directors are doing a great disservice to students if they only refer to twelve scales. This truly handicaps a student musician. Scale knowledge is the one most significant "skill exercises" in a musician's life. Scale variations are unlimited. My students never repeated a scale pattern . . . every rehearsal began with a different scale variation. I did not want to create any bad scale habits.

Musical learning is in the "doing" and the "doing" must have purpose . . . to be learned and understood. Purpose-filled learning is a process and not an event. I cannot understand why a band rehearsal begins with only the Bb concert scale. At this point in my career I have heard every possible variation of the Bb concert scale. Some bands will only use F, Bb, Eb, and possibly Ab for warm-up and tuning. This reflects the shallowness of a band program's musical training and background. Worse still, much of our published music is written in F, Bb, and Eb. When I speak with the publishers, they simply reply; "This is what the band directors are purchasing." Such a comment implies that we cannot teach all the major and minor scales. Students who graduate from such music programs are as handicapped as a high school graduate who can only read at a third-grade level. (See Appendix G for a four-step teaching process for scale mastery.)

THE GRAND MASTER SCALE

With this awareness, I changed my approach to teaching scales. I no longer referred to one scale. I coined the term "Grand Master Scale," which is *one* scale exercise that includes *all* major scales. This places scales in context with literature. In addition to the Grand Master Scale, my students had to know the Grand Master Minor Scale in the natural minor, harmonic minor, and melodic minor forms. Students no longer play scales one at a time. I refer to playing one scale at a time as being a "bad scale habit." We, as directors and teachers, taught this bad scale habit. Students must be able to respond spontaneously to any key, as literature does not stay in one key. Every accidental in a piece of music implies a new key.

Scale knowledge is crucial for a successful band program. In my publications, you will read my "Octave of Reason" for scale knowledge: scale knowledge is a student's performance vocabulary that provides the avenue for ensemble technique and articulation, sight reading skills, improvisation and creativity, spontaneous reaction to all keys, and access to a full range of band literature. This eliminates mindless repetition of technical passages, provides a foundation for harmonic understanding, and establishes pitch consistency for individual and ensemble intonation. These elements play a significant role in development of student musicians. The typical reaction to scale performance by both students and directors needs to be elevated to establish greater connections to literature.

Listed below are a few reasons for considering this instructional process for scales.

- **The Grand Master Scale establishes new musical value and worth for scale knowledge.** Scales make music. When experiencing scales in the larger context of music making, an awareness and value for such knowledge promotes greater importance for application. *Any three or more notes in a diatonic pattern imply a key.* Recognition of diatonic patterns, when reading musical notation, will eliminate a considerable amount of repetition.

- **The Grand Master Scale establishes a spontaneous reaction to all keys.** As a professional musician, I had to spontaneously relate musical notation to keys, chords, intervals, and rhythm patterns. This priority ensured sight-reading success. Using the Circle of 4ths sheet for scale performance removes the notation of scales and students create an expanded awareness to the letters for a pitch or combination of pitches. The mind creates connections as it thinks and processes the letter name as being a part of something, such as a note within a scale, melody, chord quality, or chord progression. Recognizing these all-important relationships heightens students' ability to exercise sound musical decisions.

- **The Grand Master Scale significantly improves technique throughout all sections of the band.** Performance restrictions (musical and literature) are placed upon band programs when technical skills are not consistently developed within all sections of the band. Literature standards are often compromised to overcome various section weaknesses. Playing Grand Master Scale variations daily in the warm-up process eliminates such weaknesses.

- **The Grand Master Scale eliminates mindless repetition of technical passages.** Any diatonic passage (three or more notes) implies a scale or key. There are no musical reasons to require students to practice diatonic passages found in solo or ensemble literature without connecting the passage with a scale. Unfortunately, for too many years students have played scales with limited variations (tonic to tonic in a standard rhythm pattern) and fail to recognize other scale patterns in solo or ensemble literature. Students who play scales through such a memorized habit are usually unable to *apply* such knowledge to literature if the scale passage does not start on the keynote with the practiced rhythm pattern. This creates a serious void in a student's musical skill development. (Forming a scale habit without application forms no connected meaning.)

- **The Grand Master Scale provides a meaningful approach to sight-reading.** Sight-reading is a visual reaction to notation, coupled with the spontaneous association of something previously learned with error-free application. Scanning a piece of music and associating various technical passages through scale fragments or a key eliminates a note-by-note reading process. A note-by-note reading process often produces note errors and poor rhythmic response. The eye scans and only transmits the symbol to the brain for interpretation and timed response. Scale patterns and interval recognition are important for accuracy and reading comprehension. Scale knowledge is part of our performance vocabulary for musical reading comprehension. Sight-reading is the result of teaching techniques that provide students the opportunity to apply their prior knowledge (performance vocabulary) and learned skill successfully. This is intelligent performance.

- **The Grand Master Scale provides a foundation for harmonic understanding, analysis of band literature, and a foundation for improvisation.** The state and national music standards addressing improvisation, composition, notation, and musical analysis extend teaching responsibilities and rehearsal content. The Grand Master Scale serves this purpose. It is framed in the whole of musical performance through scale, key, and harmonic relationships. Its variations and combinations allow student musicians to easily understand (hear) chord qualities and progressions, intervals, unique composer voicings (literature analysis), as well as providing an intelligent approach to classical and jazz improvisation (creativity and musical imagination).

- **The Grand Master Scale provides a foundation for solo and ensemble intonation (playing in a "pitch center").** Scales and playing an instrument in tune are *inseparable.* Playing the Grand Master Scale is critical for establishing the *in-tuneness of a melodic line*: a tonality, a feeling and hearing of in-tuneness for a particular key or its relationship to other keys. A soloist without scale performance skills has difficulty playing in tune with a band or any other form of accompaniment. Intonation problems are a result of listening to notes *out of key context or harmonic relationship.* In-tune playing is a result of pitch and melodic line connected to a given key tonality or harmonic support. Intonation is more than just the tuning note.

- **The Grand Master Scale provides access to a full range of band literature.** It is no longer necessary to compromise quality literature due to students' inability to play in various keys or scales. Too often music publications are limited to the keys of F, Bb, and Eb. Unfortunately, such limitations restrict a program's musical development. The Grand Master Scale and its variations provide the necessary technical skill to play a wide range of wind masterworks.

The Grand Master Scale is the easiest and most sure way for musical improvement. The Circle of 4ths provides a platform for unlimited scale variations for developing equal technique throughout all sections of the ensemble. I urge you to not notate the Grand Master Scale. The learning priority is to have students respond spontaneously to all keys. This is the same expectation we have for students when writing a composition or speaking . . . we do not expect them to notate and read the alphabet before they spell a word. If a student is unfamiliar with a particular scale or scales, have them sustain the tonic or key note for the duration of that scale. Expect your students to apply their scale knowledge . . . music is a language and requires a performance vocabulary.

CODA

I have attempted to express and define the myriad of musical details that are immersed in a musician's mind. The results of a musical mind are shaped through artistic interpretation of a composer's gift to an audience. Learning, understanding and appreciating the language of music shapes an individual's identity . . . a person who appreciates and respects the beauty of our world of people and art.

It was my intent to share my thoughts, perceptions, and concepts that may possibly release you and your students into a musical world never before experienced. Our musical imagination takes us into this vague, untouchable world of expressive communication, so often referred to by nonmusicians as the "magic" of music.

What is disappointing to me at this point in my career is the fact that so many school systems fail to acknowledge the importance of music study. Our programs receive tremendous support from parents while those decision makers see other "things" that are more important than making beautiful music. Are we depriving young students the opportunities to shape and respect "beauty?" A worthy band program will be designed by a creative director. Our band programs are what WE make of them, not what was handed to us. Just as we shape beautiful music with our students, we must shape our band program and move beyond the established constraints and perhaps obstacles we perceive to be in our way.

The Creative Director Series serves as a musical foundation designed to help students realize their potential for music. The system of musical learning has only been a part of music education for the past twenty years. Those who have implemented the program now experience performance levels never imagined. I experience such joy now in attending various state and national conventions and listening to the ensembles directed by those who have been a part of my clinics, workshops, and graduate sessions . . . the directors have become "creative directors."

I urge you to consider supplementing your instructional techniques through the many concepts and techniques that I have shared with you. Moreover, analyze your instructional techniques to find out what works and what doesn't. Our students are with us for a very short time. We cannot afford to consume their time with something that doesn't work even though "this is the way we always did it." Don't be afraid to question the standard operating procedures, observe the "legends" of our profession, and *read*. Everything you read, read it in the context of instrumental music. My intention with this system of musical learning is not to replace what you are doing, only to complement your program and create a greater awareness of ***why music!***

APPENDIX A.

CIRCLE OF 4THS

The Circle of 4ths Major and Minor illustration is the basis for all exercises. By applying this system, students experience the entire range of musical literature in all keys and chord qualities. Duplicate this sheet and distribute to each student.

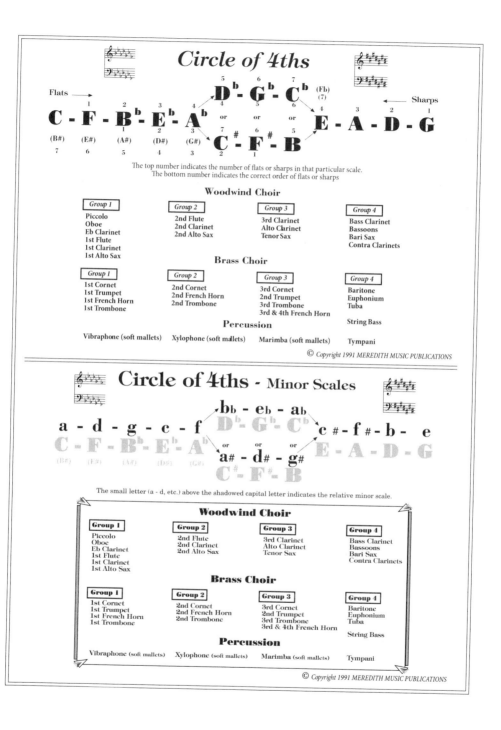

Circle of 4ths

Flats →   Sharps ←

The top number indicates the number of flats or sharps in that particular scale.
The bottom number indicates the correct order of flats or sharps

Woodwind Choir

Group 1	Group 2	Group 3	Group 4
Piccolo	2nd Flute	3rd Clarinet	Bass Clarinet
Oboe	2nd Clarinet	Alto Clarinet	Bassoons
Eb Clarinet	2nd Alto Sax	Tenor Sax	Bari Sax
1st Flute			Contra Clarinets
1st Clarinet			
1st Alto Sax			

Brass Choir

Group 1	Group 2	Group 3	Group 4
1st Cornet	2nd Cornet	3rd Cornet	Baritone
1st Trumpet	2nd French Horn	2nd Trumpet	Euphonium
1st French Horn	2nd Trombone	3rd Trombone	Tuba
1st Trombone		3rd & 4th French Horn	
			String Bass

Percussion

Vibraphone (soft mallets)   Xylophone (soft mallets)   Marimba (soft mallets)   Tympani

© Copyright 1991 MEREDITH MUSIC PUBLICATIONS

Circle of 4ths - Minor Scales

The small letter (a - d, etc.) above the shadowed capital letter indicates the relative minor scale.

Woodwind Choir

Group 1	Group 2	Group 3	Group 4
Piccolo	2nd Flute	3rd Clarinet	Bass Clarinet
Oboe	2nd Clarinet	Alto Clarinet	Bassoons
Eb Clarinet	2nd Alto Sax	Tenor Sax	Bari Sax
1st Flute			Contra Clarinets
1st Clarinet			
1st Alto Sax			

Brass Choir

Group 1	Group 2	Group 3	Group 4
1st Cornet	2nd Cornet	3rd Cornet	Baritone
1st Trumpet	2nd French Horn	2nd Trumpet	Euphonium
1st French Horn	2nd Trombone	3rd Trombone	Tuba
1st Trombone		3rd & 4th French Horn	
			String Bass

Percussion

Vibraphone (soft mallets)   Xylophone (soft mallets)   Marimba (soft mallets)   Tympani

© Copyright 1991 MEREDITH MUSIC PUBLICATIONS

APPENDIX B.

WARM-UP EXERCISES

Illustrated are several variations of exercises that will prompt and assist you in designing a rehearsal warm-up. For additional resources and variations, refer to *Student Supplement Books 1* and *2*. Apply various articulation patterns with scales as found with literature being prepared.

APPENDIX C.

SPONTANEOUS REACTION TO SCALES

Exercises are designed to develop immediate response to a key or scale by decreasing the note value of the last scale tone. This is a departure from the typical last note being a whole or half note.

APPENDIX D.

OTHER SCALE VARIATIONS

To add interest with scale performance, assign each group to begin scales as illustrated. Group 1 begins scales on Bb concert, Group 2 on F concert, Group 3 on D concert, and Group 4 on Bb concert. Students will enjoy playing three different scales at one time . . . very interesting.

With this scale variation, students will ascend the Bb, D, F, and Bb major scale and descend the chromatic scale. This is important to develop spontaneous reaction to major scale and descending chromatic scales.

This exercise illustrates scales and dynamics from piano (p) to forte (f). Groups 2, 3, and 4 will sustain whole notes while processing count 1 as piano, and count

4 as forte. To create interest and variations, change the scale pattern and assign to a weaker group, such as Group 2, 3, or 4 to increase their technical skills. Another variation can include the dynamics as being decrescendo . . . processing the dynamic as 4, 3, 2, 1.

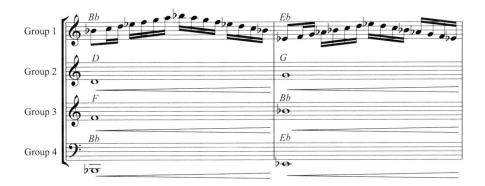

APPENDIX E.

DYNAMIC VARIATIONS

Dynamics are based on internal pulse. As each beat is silently processed the dynamic increases or decreases. This method assures equal volume expansion or contraction with every student.

Crescendo   **Decrescendo**

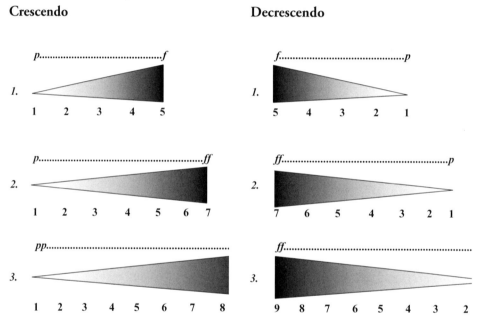

When applying this technique to method books or band literature, simply count the total number of beats (ignore bar lines or time signature) from the first indicated dynamic to the last dynamic marking. The total number of beats usually concludes as an odd-number total, which gives you the total number of beats for a *crescendo*. Count the numbers in reverse order for a *decrescendo*.

APPENDIX F.

TUNING EXERCISES

The tuning variations are critical in determining superior ensemble tone quality and sonority. Emphasis is placed on groups 3 and 4 with lesser volume with group 1.

FULL ENSEMBLE TUNING EXERCISES (Using Circle of 4ths)
Exercise Tuning in All Keys

Basic Tuning #1

Group 1: F, Bb, Eb, Ab, etc.
Group 2 & 3: C, F, Bb, Eb, etc.
Group 4: F, Bb, Eb, Ab, etc.

Tuning Variation #2

Group 1: F, Bb, F, - Bb, Eb, Bb, etc.
Group 2 & 3: C, F, C, - F, Bb, F, etc.
Group 4: F, Bb, F, - Bb, Eb, Bb, etc.
(move forward one pitch and return, etc.)

Tuning Variation #3

Group 1: F, G, F, - Bb, C, Bb, etc. (do-re-do)
Group 2 & 3: C, D, C, - F, G, F, etc. (do-re-do)
Group 4: F, G, F, - Bb, C, Bb, etc. (do-re-do)

Tuning Variation #4

Group 1: F, G, F, - Bb, A, Bb, etc. (do-ti-do)
Group 2 & 3: C, B, C, - F, G, F, etc. (do-ti-do)
Group 4: F, G, F, - Bb, A, Bb, etc. (do-ti-do)

Tuning Variation #5

Group 1: F, G, F, E, F, - Bb, C, Bb, A, Bb, etc. (*do-re-do-ti-do* or scale steps 1, 2, 1, 7, 1)
Group 2 & 3: C, D, C, B, C, - F, G, F, E, F, etc.(*do-re-do-ti-do* or scale steps 1, 2, 1, 7, 1)
Group 4: F, G, F, E, F, - Bb, C, Bb, A, Bb, etc. (*do-re-do-ti-do* or scale steps 1, 2, 1, 7, 1)

Tuning Variation #6

Group 1: F, Bb, C, Bb, F - Bb, Eb, F, Eb, Bb, etc. (*do-fa-sol-fa-do* - or scale steps 1, 4, 5, 4, 1)
Group 2 & 3: C, F, G, F, C, - F, Bb, C, Bb, F, etc. (*do-fa-sol-fa-do* - or scale steps 1, 4, 5, 4, 1)
Group 4: F, Bb, C, Bb, F - Bb, Eb, F, Eb, Bb, etc. (*do-fa-sol-fa-do* - or scale steps 1, 4, 5, 4, 1)

APPENDIX G.

SCALE MASTERY

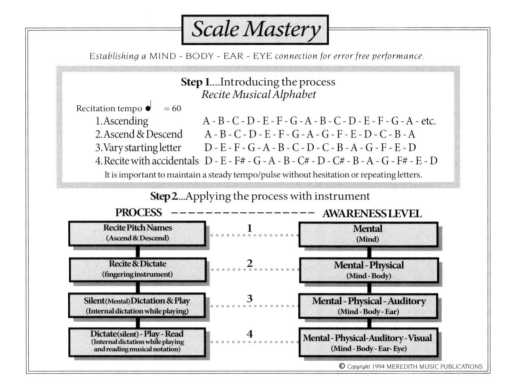

Scale Mastery

Establishing a MIND - BODY - EAR - EYE connection for error free performance.

Step 1....Introducing the process
Recite Musical Alphabet

Recitation tempo ♩ = 60
1. Ascending   A - B - C - D - E - F - G - A - B - C - D - E - F - G - A - etc.
2. Ascend & Descend   A - B - C - D - E - F - G - A - G - F - E - D - C - B - A
3. Vary starting letter   D - E - F - G - A - B - C - D - C - B - A - G - F - E - D
4. Recite with accidentals   D - E - F# - G - A - B - C# - D - C# - B - A - G - F# - E - D

It is important to maintain a steady tempo/pulse without hesitation or repeating letters.

Step 2...Applying the process with instrument

PROCESS ------------------------ AWARENESS LEVEL

PROCESS		AWARENESS LEVEL
Recite Pitch Names (Ascend & Descend)	1	**Mental** (Mind)
Recite & Dictate (fingering instrument)	2	**Mental - Physical** (Mind - Body)
Silent (Mental) **Dictation & Play** (Internal dictation while playing)	3	**Mental - Physical - Auditory** (Mind - Body - Ear)
Dictate (silent) **- Play - Read** (Internal dictation while playing and reading musical notation)	4	**Mental - Physical - Auditory - Visual** (Mind - Body - Ear - Eye)

© *Copyright* 1994 MEREDITH MUSIC PUBLICATIONS

This four-step scale mastery instructional process is based on the musical alphabet. It is different from the conventional scale teaching techniques. The process is similar to the way we learned to speak, read, and write. This simple four-step process is to be applied with learning all fifteen major scales and relative minor scales.

Scale error usually occurs in the student's mind. The conventional method does not emphasize the silent or internal speaking of the musical alphabet. This procedure ensures error-free scales the first time, while fingering the instrument and then playing the internalized alphabet with the altered scale tones. Once the student understands the four-step process, they are to apply it to every new scale. The students no longer have problems with scales as the simplicity of this natural learning process ensures correctness.

For additional resources and instructional variations, my first publication, *The Creative Director: Alternative Rehearsal Techniques*, and *Student Supplements Book 1* and *2*, have a comparatively large number of exercises. The system of musical learning is unlimited and produces a superior band program guided by a creative director.

APPENDIX H.

ARTICULATION EXERCISES

The method of articulation frequently hampers tone quality of an ensemble. As I listen to band rehearsals, the warm-up usually begins with an articulated scale. It is evident that little care is taken in the method students apply for articulation. Notes tend to be articulated in a very heavy fashion, becoming explosive at times. Rhythm patterns sound sluggish, distorted, and lose finesse and style. Articulation should always be light and never heavy, even with an accent; the heavier the tonguing, the greater the distortion of tone quality. Students must be encouraged to use the language of articulation as in ta, ti, da, di, etc. with all rhythm patterns. If they cannot articulate the pattern lightly in this manner, the results will always be sluggish and lack finesse. When I teach students, I simply state, *"If you can't say it, you can't play it."*

One of the quickest and easiest ways I developed the absolute lightness of articulation was by playing what I referred to as five-note scales: the first five notes of every scale. Playing articulated patterns in all keys provided time for the students to think about the lightness and quickness of using their tongue. I use five variations for articulation in a two-measure phrase, with the third measure sustained for a half or whole note. The five variations are as follows:

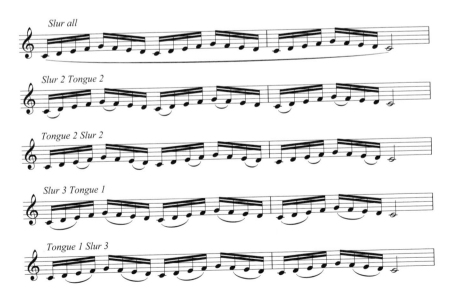

BIBLIOGRAPHY

Adler, M. (1988). *Reforming Education*. Macmillan Publishing.

Barra, D. (1983). *The Dynamic Performance*. Prentice-Hall Publications.

Bartholomew, W. (1942). *Acoustics of Music*. Prentice-Hall, Inc.

Battisti, F. (2007). *On Becoming a Conductor*. Meredith Music Publications, distributed by Hal Leonard, Inc.

Blum, D. (1977). *Casals and the Art of Interpretation*. University of California Press.

Copland, A. (1980). *Music and Imagination*. Harvard University Press.

Csikszentmihalyi, M. (1996). *Creativity*. HarperCollins Publishers.

Csikszentmihalyi, M. (1990). *Flow: The Psychology of Optimal Experience*. Harper & Row, Publishers.

Csikszentmihalyi, M. (1994). *The Evolving Self: A Psychology for the Third Millennium*. Harper Perennial.

Gardner, H. (1982). *Art, Mind & Brain: A Cognitive Approach to Creativity*. Basic Books, Inc.

Gardner, H. (1983). *Frames of Mind: The Theory of Multiple Intelligences*. Basic Books, Inc.

Gazzaniga, M. (2008). *Human: The Science Behind What Makes Us Unique*. HarperCollins Publishers.

Gordon, E. (2003). *Learning Sequences in Music: Skill Content and Patterns*. GIA Publications.

Green, B. (2004). *The Mastery of Music: Ten Pathways to True Artistry*. GIA Publications.

Jensen, E. (1998). *Teaching With the Brain in Mind*. ASCD Publications.

Jordan, J. (1999). *The Musician's Soul*. GIA Publications.

Jourdain, R. (1997). *Music, the Brain, and Ecstasy*. New York: William Morrow & Company, Inc.

Lazear, D. (1991). *Seven Ways of Knowing*. Skylight Publishing.

Levitin, D. (2007). *This Is Your Brain on Music*. Plume/Penguin Group, Inc.

Lisk, E. (1991). *The Creative Director: Alternative Rehearsal Techniques*. Meredith Music Publications, distributed by Hal Leonard, Inc.

Lisk, E. (1996). *The Intangibles of Musical Performance*. Meredith Music Publications, distributed by Hal Leonard, Inc.

Lisk. E. (2006). *The Creative Director: Conductor, Teacher, Leader*. Meredith Music Publications, distributed by Hal Leonard, Inc.

Lisk, E. (2001). *The Creative Director: Beginning & Intermediate Levels*. Meredith Music Publications, distributed by Hal Leonard, Inc.

Lisk, E. (1993). *The Creative Director: Student Supplements Books 1 & 2*. Meredith Music Publications, distributed by Hal Leonard, Inc.

Miles, R. (1997). *Teaching Music Through Performance in Band (8 Volumes)*. GIA Publications.

Restak. R. (1988). *The Mind*. Bantam Books.

Russell, P. (1979). *The Brain Book*. E. P. Dutton, Inc.

Sloboda, J. (2005). *Exploring the Musical Mind*. Oxford University Press.

Sylwester, R. (1995). *A Celebration of Neurons: An Educator's Guide to the Human Brain*. ASCD Publications.

Wilson, F. (1986). *Tone Deaf and All Thumbs?* Viking Penguin, Inc.

About the Author

Called a "unique leader in the profession" and "a dynamic force in music education," Edward S. Lisk has been invited to speak and conduct throughout the United States and abroad. He is the author of numerous critically acclaimed best-selling books and editor of the *Edwin Franko Goldman March* Series for Carl Fisher Music Publications, and coauthor of GIA publications *Teaching Music Through Performance in Band* (8 volumes). His many honors and awards include the *National Band Hall of Fame for Distinguished Conductors,* the *2009 Midwest Medal of Honor,* and past president (2000) of the American Bandmasters Association. A highly sought after clinician, conductor, and speaker, he serves on the board of directors of the Midwest Clinic and the John Philip Sousa Foundation. He lives in Oswego, New York with his wife Dorie.

ADDITIONAL TITLES BY EDWARD S. LISK:

The Creative Director: Alternative Rehearsal Techniques
Copyright © 1991
ISBN: 0-9624308-0-3

The Creative Director: Intangibles of Musical Performance
Copyright © 1996
ISBN: 0-9624308-5-4

The Creative Director: Conductor, Teacher, Leader
Copyright © 2006
ISBN-13: 978-1-57463-079-4
ISBN-10: 1-57463-079-2

The Creative Director: Beginning and Intermediate Levels
Copyright © 2001
ISBN: 0-634-03044-2

Student Supplement, Book I
Copyright © 1993
ISBN: 0-9624308-1-1

Student Supplement, Book II
Copyright © 1994
ISBN: 0-9624308-2-X

The Creative Director: Alternative Rehearsal Techniques
Teaching Accessories
Copyright © 1995
ISBN: 0-9624308-3-8

DVD: Alternative Rehearsal Techniques
Virginia Commonwealth University Wind Ensemble
Edward S. Lisk, Clinician; Dr. Terry Austin, Director
Copyright © 1994
ISBN: 0-9624308-4-6

The Creative Director Series publications are distributed by:
Hal Leonard Corporation
7777 W. Bluemound Rd.
Milwaukee, WI 53213
414-774-3630
www.meredithmusic.com